EMBRACE THE WARRIOR WITHIN

A Rollercoaster Ride That's Guaranteed
to Keep You Hooked

MILLY JONES

authorHOUSE®

AuthorHouse™ UK
1663 Liberty Drive
Bloomington, IN 47403 USA
www.authorhouse.co.uk
Phone: 0800.197.4150

Published by AuthorHouse 02/13/2019

ISBN: 978-1-7283-8467-2 (sc)
ISBN: 978-1-7283-8466-5 (e)

Print information available on the last page.

Any people depicted in stock imagery provided by Getty Images are models,
and such images are being used for illustrative purposes only.
Certain stock imagery © Getty Images.

This book is printed on acid-free paper.

CONTENTS

EMBRACE THE WARRIOR WITHIN

This adventure book is my experience of living with and surviving a Mental Health illness. Travelling through manic highs and depressive lows; this book takes you on the rollacoaster ride of my life. Using poetry and "snippets of my mind" I unveil myself to the public and embrace the hand I was given.

Mental health issues have hit me hard and so this book is here to inspire people. It's hard, but you have to carry on through the ups and downs and pick yourself up whenever you fall. Because despite coming back from the darkest of places, I can now say I AM HAPPY TO BE ALIVE.

INTRODUCTION

I have wanted to write a book for quite a while but kept pulling out, believing I have nothing interesting to say. I wanted to make the book meaningful, descriptive, a book that had some kind of point for other people and myself. I felt that every time I came to write, words came out as a load of nonsense, never actually fully explaining anything I wanted to, or how I felt about what goes on in my life. For some reason, I felt I needed to prove to the outside world and to myself, that what I experience was worth writing about and not necessarily the norm. Another reason is that I had a strong belief that I needed to live up to other people expectations, even though I am unsure what these were, or in fact are. For a while, I couldn't see or understand why anyone would care about my life or what I felt. As a person, I have low self-esteem and find it difficult talking about myself and the experiences I go through on a daily basis. I am certainly not a celebrity, nor am I a special person with an important life. I am like you, and everyone else, just trying to make my way in the world with the hand I have been dealt.

In May 2013, I decided to begin a blog of living with the diagnosis of Rapid Cycle Bipolar Disorder. At first I was only able to share the web address with my close family and friends but I was overwhelmed to receive such a beautiful reaction from the people who were so close to me. This inevitably lead to me write more and more with my secret life being opened up. People were finally starting to see the side of me which I hid for so long. Although most recognized I had mental health problems, they did not understand to what extent and this new blog became my connection to the outside world. Growing in confidence, it took me a year, but in March 2014, I released my blog web address on Facebook. Again, the reaction I received was phenomenal. I got so many heart-warming messages saying how strong I was and how I was an inspiration to others. As the wheel began turning, I became comfortable enough to show my writing to my care-coordinator, Kate and support workers at a local mental health support charity. I was overwhelmed again with the feedback from everyone and writing quickly became my first line of expression. I have since had a poem published on the Black Dog website and writing put up at my local Support charity.

Encouraged by my blog response and the joy and understanding my writing brings others; I have decided to put together this book. I get such joy from writing, and it is my internal release. I hope within sections of this book people can gain an understanding of it is like to live with a mental health illness and the demons it brings. In turn, I hope people who experience the same difficulties find comfort in the fact they are not alone. I am a determined person, and never give up, no matter what life seems to throw at me. I hope this comes across but moreover that it inspires other people to keep going through it all.

The following book covers my life from leaving sixth from and getting mixed diagnosis until the age of 29. I am on a complex journey, which I am just starting to accept and move forward with, knowing I will always be that bit different. The book is set out in chapters of my life and follows through with 'snippets into my mind' that represent the bizarre things I experience. The book maybe a bit hectic, but this is my life and I cannot write any other way.

<u>Enjoy!</u>

PROFILE

My name is Milly Jones. I am a 25 to 29-year-old female at the writing of this book and live in Yorkshire, England. I come from a normal family life, with two older brothers who I get on with well and a Mother and Father who love me dearly. At the moment I am living at the Priory Hospital on a rehab ward in England. I have been here for almost a year and am proud to say I have a discharge date for the 23rd April 2018. Four years ago I was back living at home with the support of parents as carers and seeing one of my brothers regularly. The other lives in Canada with his wife and children, whom we communicate with via skype or what's app trying to visit as much as we can.

I had a normal upbringing, seeing my grandparents regularly and playing out with friends every evening. I used to be a dancer, joining in with show performances at the local theatre and taking part in exams. I loved being activate as a child and would often be out the house with friends or family in the streets. This continued throughout high school, where I had a brilliant set of mates and we had many a drunken party at the weekend and trips to the Lakes in the later years. All I remember of this time is being worry free and laughing at everything. During my younger years of high school we used to have a group called GMUIZ, which is a Chinese word for family. We would dress up as sumo wrestlers at sleepovers, stuffing pillows up our tops and play fighting. Life with my friends at high school was pretty prefect. There was no bitching, as we were a mixed gender group.

Fortunately, we were in no way naughty kids and most of us held down simple shop jobs during our teen years. I was not one of the popular kids at school; however I just seemed to get one with everyone. I have suffered from dyslexia throughout my life, leaving me in lower classes and putting me down in my English. I did not let this defeat me, going on the study A-levels, then to try university and to write this book. However, sixth from is where things began to go wrong. I began hearing voices and having an unstable mood. Here begins my first chapter: experiencing the knowledge that something was not quite right.

SIXTH FORM - WHERE THINGS BEGAN TO GO WRONG

Mental illness can hit anyone, of any background, age or gender. I am not going to lie and say I have had a difficult childhood; it was in fact quite normal and enjoyable. I loved primary school and high school: lots of friends and lots of laughs. It was not until sixth form that the devils and demons decided to pay a visit. Sticking around like an unwanted smell, these demons played havoc with my head and messed with my moods, creating a huge mood rollacoaster, which I was unable to escape. It is not until now, writing this book and looking back, I realise how strong I am and what I have been though.

Seventeen was where it all started: all went downhill. I entered sixth form with eleven GCSE's and began to study Psychology, Religious Studies and Biology A Levels. I quickly found the work a lot harder than high school, and that my dyslexic diagnosis was making things more difficult. I dropped Biology at the end of the first year, without a qualification, and took History up as an AS Level in second year. Again, things began to get too much and I was forced to drop out a few weeks later. Looking back I can clearly see this is where by identity confusion, the course changes started and mental illness combined with stress became a real issue in my life.

Sixth form was anything but smooth sailing, the mood and personality changes began, and the voices started with paranoia setting in. However, I was out nearly every weekend, drunk in town or out at parties. Maybe I appeared like a normal teenager on the outside, to onlookers, but inside I was struggling. Struggling to want to be alive, to act normal and to keep breathing and keep control. I guess I wanted to and had to hide my struggle for most people around me. Depression had hit me hard, and whilst others my age where finding their way in life, I was struggling just to get though the day. Dark clouds covered my every move and tinted what joy I found whilst trying to remain normal. I had to begin to adapt clothing to hide my arms, as self-harm had made its way into my life. Taking away my confidence, I began to look silently odd on night outs, as I was forced into my own style combination of long sleeves. I was keen to go out most weekends, drinking to forget my pain, however this often led to fits as my emotional body turned my pain physical. My friends did not care though; they accepted me as me and stuck by my side, although this was only the tip of the iceberg.

Unfortunately, my symptoms become more severe as time went on, as they kept creeping up on me, making their way through my body as if they belonged. Deeper depression and hearing voices hit me as a tidal waves as I was just beginning to challenge myself in my teenage years: in hindsight having a devastating impact on my now adult life. Whilst attending college I would be thrown into states of semi-consciousness, hysterically crying and having voices shouting abuse at me. I was completely unaware of what was going on at the time, thinking they were panic attacks and normal. They would come out of the blue and I was unaware of any triggers that would bring on such violent attacks. I wanted; needed to, act on my voices that were chanting evil and disturbing things about my life and others. My tutors were extremely supportive and became my lifeline throughout college. They would sit with me until I came around and spent hours talking to me. I got extremely close to both my Psychology Tutor and my Learning Support Tutor. I regret not being able to keep into touch with my Psychology Tutor, because she was amazing, and I am sure that she will never know how she literally kept me alive through those two years. She was always there for me; listened when there was no one to turn to and had none judgement comment about my situation. I told her more than I had ever told anyone else at the time, so to lose touch is sad, but I suppose as my Tutor, inevitable. As to my Learning Support Tutor, she always taught me never to give up, no matter what life throws at you. A motto I have always clung on to and tried to live by.

So depression had got its claws in rather bad in the second year of sixth form. You could see it in my eyes, hear it in my voice and feel it in the air around me. I began to separate myself from my friends believing they were plotting against me, out to kill me. The voices I heard were evil but I could not separate them from reality. I seemed to be keeping one eye closed and the other in life. I kept close with one friend whom I went with on drives to pet shops and supermarkets. Again, I am not sure he relates how close we were to how he kept me alive at the time. That's the thing of growing up with a mental illness, simple friendships can mean so much and actually help you to keep going. That friend will often never know or understand their impact on your life or how they have kept you alive and breathing for longer than you personally wanted.

Fortunately and unfortunately, I was excellent and hiding my mental health struggles and seeming well. A smile on my face: a tear in my eye: a mask that only some people knew what was behind. Many of my family were unaware of the impact of the voices I heard, or even their severity. They saw their princess who was stolen in the night and replaced by depression monster who began to withdraw from the world. Looking back, and talking to my parents, I don't think they or I realised how bad it was, we were both as confused as each other.

I remember the moment I finally had the courage to tell my mum about the self-harming, not a pleasant conversation. It was revealed in the only way possible- drunk. I had just been on a night out, had a fit, and a disconnecting episode of semi-consciousness when she picked me up at two in the morning. I cried all way home and then blurted it out when we arrived, showing her the mess that was now my arms. I think we cried together but I cannot remember what fully happened, her reaction or the after consequences.

This is now my life of disconnecting, not remembering things from my past. So to write these memories ten years on is hard because my mind and inner voices will not allow it. This will be a theme though out the book, although I try hard to remember, some things are just impossible: A survival technique gone wrong.

It was my Learning Support Tutor who first took me to my GP for my 'panic attack' and voices suggesting they were not normal. I was then referred to the Early Intervention Team (EIT) via the CMHT and diagnosised with Depression and Psychosis. All my life I had seen a young girl in the corner of rooms who others could not see and have always had multiple voices inside my head. Although the outside voices were new, it was not until I attended these EIT appointments that I realised that none of this was normal. I can not remember the ins and outs of my involvement with EIT but can remember I went with a college assistant for a few times to meet my new care coordinator. I had not told my family of my visit or appointments, feeling embarrassed by the situation and a need to protect them. This made college my one and only contact point. I then began to see my care co-ordinator at least once a week on an individual basis, talking through my symptoms. I also went under a Psychiatrist who I began to see at least every 3 months. My Care coordinator was nice on principle, but is not something I wish to delve into, as my memory of her is very mixed.

I think a lot was explained to me at the time but I was too ill to understand, to embarrassed to tell my parents. To be honest, I can not remember much of that time of being ill any more, or what people did for me. It not only hurts to remember but also that I can't. There is a blank space of that time of my life, like it did not happen.

Eventually, l was admitted to Underwood, a Mental Health Hospital, for 3 weeks as an inpatient and 2 weeks on leave. All my friends and family took time to visit me in Hospital, which to this day I am grateful for. They came to play games and to chat about life; we did not talk about being ill nor was I judged. Everyone I knew stuck by my side and these people have never left.

Looking back, this is a remarkable thing to do for my friends who were only 17 or 18 at the time. It must have been difficult for them; to visit someone they had grown up with in an adult psychiatric hospital. The place was rather scary, with people shouting and many psychotic patients that we had only observed in films. I had began to isolate myself quite badly the weeks before being admitted, and to this day I am unsure what they thought was going on, but none of this stopped them from visiting me. I am so proud to call them my friends, and 10 years on we are still so close and keep in touch. I love them all to bits, which will be covered in a later chapter.

Unfortunately, as you can tell everything hit rock bottom whilst I was taking my A level

exams and completing course work. In the end, I only managed to complete two A levels in Psychology and Religious Studies. Remarkably however, I managed to achieve C's for each and an AS Level in General Studies. This was enough to gain me a place at my first choice university for September starting 2007. Unlike others on results day, I also had an outpatient's appointment at the hospital and was still under their care. Craziness was never too far away. Unfortunately, I was not discharged but I had a smile on my face and went for a BBQ with friends knowing I was still technically under hospital mental health care. This then began to become my secret life. I often spent my time trying to remain normal, seeing my friends and revising, whilst also seeing a care coordinator with EIT and keeping out of hospital. Looking back, I have no idea how I have managed to get though it all. It is all such a blur. But I did, and magically did not alienate my friends who I was so paranoid of.

After being discharged from hospital in the August, I went to University late September. That is when the bubble really burst and everything really fell apart. I am undecided whether it was a good idea to go to university or not. I was still rather ill at the time but I did not want to be left alone to ruminate and mull things over. I would have been left behind whilst all of my friends moved on, my life lines moved on, and that was not something I would stand for. So I did, I went. My life continued like any other teenager as I carried on through in to my first university year.

As a result of having severe depression as a teen, an old care coordinator, Kate, once said that this had taken away my coping strategies that are formed for adult life. Therefore, as well as coping with my current diagnosis and current life symptoms, I am fighting hard to try to learn how to cope with everyday life. Being a teenager is hard, challenging your boundaries and trying to find yourself. Having to cope with Psychosis and Depression on top meant those core understanding of living was hard to learn as well. Some of these didn't catch on at all. For a while I was struggling to gain the normality, which was lost at 17.

SNIPPET INTO MY MIND - SELF-HARM

Do you ever get that tense up feeling in your body? Although nothing has happened, you need some way to escape the pain that's building up inside you. So you go to bizarre lengths to let out that pain by physically harming yourself. It makes no sense afterwards but right then in that moment in time, it is the only way to let the burning monsters inside you out. It is like a craving, a craving to release all the tense up feeling inside. You know once you draw that blade down to your skin that the endorphins will release and you will start to feel better. You can then forget all the other pain, the emotional pain, as your body, your mind had something new to focus on.

Self-harm enters your life and trust me, that demon that will never leave!

UNDERWOOD - A POEM – AGED 18

The following poem I wrote whilst in hospital in 2007. I was a keen writer at the time filling many notebooks with random scribbles. Lots of things written in them are so illegible as they discuss what the voices were saying during this period. This poem was readable and helps explain my feelings around being locked away and my life being taken away.

Eighteen and I have been locked away
What did I do, what did I say

Who are these people who have forced me inside
Aggravating my voices, taking my pride

Nobody has explained anything to myself
Just that they are protecting me and my health

I don't know what I did, or how I have acted
But locked up away, over reacted

I am not ill, there is nothing wrong with me
Just look into my eyes and let me free

These four walls have trapped me for a month
But I don't feel any better, I don't feel a pulse

I want to die, so they have locked me away
Saying I am psychotic, stay another day

Eighteen and I am losing my life
Will it get better, Will I get out

Underwood was not a nice place to be in at 18. Looking back, I cannot remember much of my time there, just being fed, having a bedtime and being focus fed medication. Luckily, I was discharged after a total of five weeks but prayed that I would never go back. At the time I was then able to enjoy some of the last few weeks of summer with my mates and have a good send off into the world of university.

UNIVERSITY NUMBER ONE - OUT OF HOSPITAL, INTO THE DEEP

The first year at university was rather hectic to say the least. I found myself "studying" 5 different university courses through various course changes. The psychosis was beginning to become under control via medication and I was on an antidepressant for the low mood. However, what was in stall was a rollacoaster ride of a different kind, resulting in periods of extreme highs and extreme lows for weeks on end. Battling to keep my head above water, my mood took control of my life and I began to give in to my mental illness.

At the beginning I settled in rather well to university life. Being two hours from home, I did not feel too separated from my former life and travelling home was easy. I chose a quite, campus University to do a joint degree in Theology and Psychology: both my former A Levels. I love the place, with squire's running around the campus and the city only a short walk away. From Lancashire, I am a country girl and dislike big cities, so a small campus university was in a perfect compact city, with a guarding wall and unique old style building. I moved into a house with 26 girls and quickly made friends with the girls on my floor. At time I thought this was amazing but the friendships soon became hard to handle, as my mental illness took control.

There were nine of us altogether in our group and we mostly got on well. I had come from a group of friends that never bitched or fell out, so adjusting to being with a group of nine girls was hard and eventful. There seemed to be more bitching going on at university than I had experienced through my whole time at high school. This was not something I expected. The group quickly became suffocating and I began to get ridiculed for my extreme moods, as they did not understand. A bunch of five of us managed to kind of break off, but we still remain together, buying a house in our second year. It wasn't all bad though, we had some brilliant times together, going out on student nights out, gambling at the races and having take away nights in.

At the time, I was unwilling to admit that anything was wrong with me, so never talked about my difficulties with these new friends. They did not know about my past, about hospital or my struggle with my mental illness. However, only a couple of months into the first term, a friend approached me, saying my moods were unstable and I was often unpredictable. I know I used to enjoy spending whole nights out in a row in the town getting drunk and surviving on a couple of hours sleep. I also know I had spending sprees like no students should. However, I also spent half my time just sitting in my bedroom crying, or being taken home to 'recuperate'. I thought this was normal, the extreme of going out and getting tired after months of being on the go. Only now do I recognize it was more than this, and those none stop thoughts and waking people up to go on walks with me at 4 in morning were a product of mania, not normal student behaviour.

My friends were good though, and as I said we had some good times. Although there was some bitchiness, we never really fell out, I think it was just the result of being a group of girls. The problem was that they didn't understand. They had not experienced someone with such mental health issues before. My home friends knew me as me first, until the addition of my twin demon. These new people just knew me as a whole, demon included. I do not resent them for the fact. They were 18, taking their own first steps into an independent life, why should they know or accept mental illness this way. However, this is where the damage took place, apart from one person; they could not separate this side of me. So they bitched and my paranoid set in again.

I would like to point out here though, that I had some hard times at University and my friends stood by me. I required frequent visits to A&E where my new friends would sit with me for hours waiting to see the psychiatrist. I used to become semi-conscious, hysterically cry and talk incoherent language, like in sixth from. On several occasions this scared staff and friends enough to take me to hospital to keep me safe. I am ever so grateful for this care, even with their lack of understanding our friendship did have a level of a caring connection.

Only now as I look back do I recognise these periods as dissociation. It is beginning to scare me writing this book of how long things have been going on for. The language and semi consciousness is now attributed to another diagnosis, which has been happening for a lot longer than I have thought.

Unfortunately, I left University, with only one real friend. A friend who will always be there, even when we don't talk for months or even a year she would be the same if I was to phone her up. Luckily, she managed to break free from this group too, after a hard time settling in to her second year. I don't regret making these friends, as they were nice people, but for my situation and me they were not right. In the end, they bullied me out of university and we haven't been in contact since.

Over my year at university, my rollacoaster of the mood changes set in more and more. There became chances to be free and chances to dance with the sun. New ideas formed in my head, which in turn created new parts of me and paths that my life could now take. Of course, when the sun was around, I thought I was of higher intellect then anyone around at the time and could do anything; even trying to fly on several occasions. Everything seemed so open and so possible with this strong self-belief. To be honest, I don't understand why they let me change so much, but they did and I thought it was the best thing ever. In the end I started five separate university courses at the University in one year. These were: Psychology, Theology, Counselling Skills, Criminology and Religious Studies. I then began Theology again as a first year, when others were going into their second. This did not last.

I think during University and the times of my mood changes, I began not to think of my life as a whole, instead to live as separate parts, either with the mania or the depression. I wasn't sure why I was a fun loving girl one minute and crying my eyes out the next, but it didn't matter. Not to me, but apparently it did to my friendships, to my courses and indeed my life. I seemed to be changing so much week by week that the lovable me began to be snatched in the night then replaced a few weeks later. The voices and depression kept coming as if out of nowhere and change how I thought and how I acted. They took a part of me away, each time and I had to learn to bond with the chatter in my head and cope with my difficulties; changing course seem the right way.

In the end, it meant that my moods started to create a weather rollacoaster that I don't think anyone would like to be on, or as I found out, to be around. I began hiding my mood the best I could and I thought I was doing well, in hindsight this may not be too true and friendships started to dwindle with others, not just those in our group. I think it became hard for friends to understand my rollacoaster so I began to push them away and they began too push me away to, making my life so much harder. As a result I began to separate my new lifestyles and tried to keep a cap on my moods keeping the view that everything was fine.

Whilst all this was going on, I was still living my secret life, which I formed in sixth form. I was semi transferred to the local EIT but was still under my old care coordinator for some time. Still on my antidepressant and Risperidone -an anti psychotic, I thought the medication was working extremely well. The voices, to some degree, begin to diminish but hallucinations had set in. Although as mentioned, I had times of semi consciousness, my moods were my main issues through university as they were something I could remember and observed by others. I had a new care-coordinator for a few months during the end of my time at university, but often I would see the local GP who was brilliant with me.

In May 2008 things finally got too much and I took an overdose at university. Luckily I escaped without damage and my friend Darcy stood by me through it all. Singing 'life is a flower, so whilst down the wind' whilst I was in hospital got me through and I still remember it to this day. Given the time space of nearly fifteen years since the overdose, I still do not regret my action. I supposed I wanted to die, and that would have been dreadful, but at the same time, it was a cry for help. It seemed to be the last straw with friendships and I was able to move on more easily. I did return for September 2008 to start Theology, but nothing was the same, and looking back, I am now thankful. The overdose was a blessing in disguise; I really must not have been coping well to taken one. It is strange to view it as this and I have only just realised what impact it actually had to ending my time at the University.

So I moved home in October 2008, bought a bunny rabbit called Jo-Jo and went to Canada for a month to visit my brother. It gave me time to reflect on my past, and indeed my future and see how I now could start to move forwards. Positively I did and the next few years I remain well.

SNIPPET INTO MY HEAD - VOICES AND MUDDLED THOUGHTS

All my life I have wanted to learn to like myself. I don't want to listen to the voices inside my head and the lies they tell. It is so hard to try and move on. I want to talk about what people say to me, what running commentary I have going on in my head. How everyday I don't believe what I think and have to force the voices to shut up to function. I am trying so hard to move my life on and try and force the evil voices away. But as I do I am reminded by periods of semi-consciousness and loss of voice, which just aggravate my voices inside and out further. I guess I need to talk about things I cannot let out. I feel I have so many secrets, which I cannot tell in my head never mind out loud. I hate myself so much that I don't even want to get better. It feels so painful to admit.

I cannot understand how nothing was out of ordinary in childhood to cause such distress in this later life. Why can't I complete one year at university? I loved school; I love to study. I would love to have the feeling that I wanted to live and that I did not have a suicide plan all the time. How do I take away the pain, the voices, and the hallucinations? I'm fighting so hard to gain a normal life but it feels too far away. It feels I am like going on a bear hunt. I have to move all the other voices, strange thoughts and beliefs out my head just to function normally. The happy ones that want to play all the time and stay up all night. And the dark voices who want to hide. Nothing is helping me fight the battle but my brain is all muddled. I want more than anything to stay stable and I am battling so much. I want to know what make things so hard and why I am finding it so difficult to process things. I need to learn my triggers in life and where the separation between where my alternate universe and I lies.

RETURNING TO HOME, RETURNING TO WORK, RETURNING TO NORMAL

I thought that moving home would be the hardest thing in the world but I must admit, again, that I am unsure of the exact details on moving out. I knew I was no longer a student or indeed anyone that could give anything to life. This was hard to deal with, as I had to settle back in at home. With my friends all enjoying their second year, I was once again looking to find the right path for my life.

EIT had left me without a discharge letter, or in fact telling me that they were discharging me. I felt so alone and didn't know which way to turn. I felt I had regressed back and hadn't moved on from a year ago. Luckily, my mood had started to stable out, and an increase in Risperidone started to help. I had a brilliant relationship with my GP so was able to visit him if I need anything, literarily anything.

So here I was, back home, boxes around the house, bedroom a mess and no idea where to put anything, or in fact where to start again. To clear my head I decided to go to Canada for a few weeks to stay with my brother. This, in hindsight was the best decision ever. I was able to separate things out and take a full look over my life and where I wanted it to go.

Vancouver is where he lives, with his former wife and two children. It was just he and his wife at the time I visited and they worked through the week leaving me to do my own things. They lived in a flat, just off the main street of Vancouver centre, so access was brilliant. I spent my days chilling in Coffee shops and walking around Stanley Park. It was beautiful weather and the fresh air combined with coffee really gave me time to clear my head.

Feeling confident I was able to organise, two trips out on my own. The first was to Seattle and the other to Whistler. I went to Seattle with my brother and his wife, to go shopping in America first. It was all very exciting, and I decided to challenge myself and book a night in a local hostel in Seattle centre. To this day l am proud that I achieved this, and although terrified and cried myself to sleep, I was taking one of my biggest steps to independence. I have to remember; I was only nineteen and at the time and I had already been through so much, so that night is something I am grateful for. I then happily spent one day on my own, travelling on a DUCK tour and walking around the city centre. I caught the greyhound bus back with a smile on my face and glean in my eye.

My second trip was not as extreme but meant so much to me on a personal level. I took it upon myself to organise a day trip to Whistler, catching the greyhound there and back from Vancouver. I spent my day watching the mountain bikers come down the slopes in which l had skied just a few years before. Reminiscing, I could still feel the hurt from that ski trip which I had taken with my family. It was when I was going though a bad stage of depression and when breathing was hard. But as I sat there with the sun on my face, watching everyone, my pulse hit me and I knew I had to start making plans to move forward. It was not big or dramatic, just a sense that I was alive and ready to move on. I can still remember this feeling to this day and considered it an important step in my recovery and the chance to change my path. As I travelled home on the bus I remember feeling so small in between the huge mountains. For the first time in years I felt at peace and ready to move towards a new life, with new beginnings and new adventures.

So that's what I did. I came home, stated planning for future and applying for jobs. Luckily, a plan had started to grow in my head. On the plane on the way home, whilst sat next to a drunken guy who kept offering me whiskey, I made a decision that the health care route was the way for me. At home I began applying for healthcare assistant jobs at the local hospital and to be fair, anything in that relative field. I quickly discovered I needed more experience but did not give up easily. I also found, that my now scared arms were going to be a problem. I had stopped self-harming for about three months and this was the push to give up altogether. Neither arms nor experience were going to stop me in my new adventures. My mum worked in the Pathology department at our local hospital and noticed a job was coming up in Central Specimen Reception, CSR as a Medical Laboratory Assistant. I applied, had a successful interview and started work in January 2009.

By this time my moods were relatively stable. They had settled down to a nice flow, often more extreme than others but without the devastating destruction. My psychotic symptoms were also being well controlled with Risperidone. For this time, I was not under any mental health team and only visited my doctors on occasions. This in turn meant I no longer had a secret life to lead, or hidden demons to hide. I began working 8-hour shifts, 12-8, five days a week and loved it. I walked my dog every morning, lost a lot of weight and felt happier in myself. Work was great, I made some amazing new friends and everyday was a great laugh. My job included receiving blood specimens from outpatients, the wards and GP practices. Tests were then coded up and the bloods spun down in the centrifuge ready for testing at other departments. Everyone was really friendly and we all got on very well.

I began working in the week and living for my weekends. During the summer of 2009 I spent most at my free time and weekends out on the town, partying it up with my best friend, Jenny, and brother, Mark. We were having the best of times, attending work and friend parties and BBQs. I felt so included and alive at that point in time and still feel that it was the best summer of my life to date. I was no longer having the fits or episodes of semi-consciousness that I had had at sixth form and my body felt so alive without any extreme moods like at University. I was finally joining in with the mellow party of life. However, I was also beginning to get itchy feet and wanted to challenge myself more, so the planning stages set in again, and the wheel started turning.

Now being a happier person, I decided I was ready to go back to university. Although I loved my job, I am also an academic person and love to study. I started researching local courses and found an Occupational Therapy course at local University. This was perfect. Only 40 minuets away, I felt I wouldn't have the same pressures as before, by moving so far away if things went wrong again. So, I applied, had another successful interview and became accepted late August 2009. I then started the OT course in October. I crossed my fingers and hoped this was the right path for my life, jumping in headfirst. Overall, what year I had had and I was hoping it would continue.

SECOND UNIVERSITY - OCCUPATIONAL THERAPY AND THE LIVING YEARS

My first year at my second University was a success. I left the NHS and the pathology department behind in late August and moved to my second university in the last week of September 2009. Nervously, I packed up all my belonging again, kitchen things that I had bought previously, and boxes that were never unpacked from the last year. My parents took me in their car and we headed down the A6 to my new home. My heart was pounding, wondering whether I was doing the right thing. Course number six, University number two. I think I had more worries than the avenge student that day, but I remember all the smiling faces as we arrived and the support we received on freshets week. I soon knew I had made the right decision.

Somewhere inside of me I was excited, ready to move on and felt 18 again starting university for the first time. Unfortunately, this feeling did not last, but not necessarily in a bad way. I found I was living in a flat with a group of girls including me, most of whom were 18 and the other girl who was luckily my age, and on my course. Feeling 18 and being 18, I found out is a little different. These girls liked to party, a lot. They played loud music till silly o'clock and rolled in loud and drunk late. This is typical of early student life which I had already experienced I did not mind, as this was I just two years before, but it did make me feel old at only twenty. All the girls were lovely, and we got on well. However, Joy and I found our selves going home each weekend to get some peace and quiet. How old were we!

Another main difference between us two, and the flat girls, was we were on a professional qualification course and so couldn't mess around as much. I am in no means saying we were boring, we just had a lot more work to do than they seemed to. All this said, we were out partying whenever we could, going into town and in to clubs where we quickly became good friends with a group of girls from our OT course. Strangely enough though, as our age set in we were buying salad pittas instead of chips on a night out. Funny things like that make you feel a bit older than the tiny eighteen year old flat girls who were always on chips. Luckily for me, this course attracted older students then 18 years olds, which actually meant I was one of the younger student in our class. In addition, some people had been to university before, so like me were not necessarily there just to get drunk all the time, as they too had already had the student life.

As the course started everyone was so friendly, but like always people separated off into smaller groups. We had a group of eight of us in our group, who were really close and would meet up regularly. We sat together in classes and lectures and would communicate a lot out of university, meeting up and going for meals or nights out. There was none of the bitchness that I experienced in before. OT was a good course and most days involved group work so the whole class got to know each other and we bonded really well. Even to this day, five years on I still speak to people I met on that first day; I guess that is thanks to social media.

OT was a great course and I thoroughly enjoyed my first year. It was a lot harder than the other course I had 'studied' and required a lot more independent research. In our first year we had a test called VIVA. In this we had to research for ourselves and learn 10 questions over two months on anatomy of the body. We would then have to pick two at random and talk about them for five minutes each to a tutor, being assessed on what we had learned and remembered. It was a stressful time; probably the most stress I had been under for a while. But I got though and passed with a 2.1 on that module. No demons appeared.

In the first year of the course also included two placements, one at the beginning that was an observational placement and a 6-week one near the end of the first year. For my six-week placement I was lucky enough to go an Older Adults Mental Health ward. I thoroughly enjoyed this placement and got close to my educator who was brilliant. I was committed to becoming an OT and loving the skills I was learning. I felt for the first time in life, natural at something and knew this pathway was for me. In addition, I did well on my placement and did not want to leave. I loved my time there and loved being and calling myself an OT.

University life was going brilliantly too. The friends I had made were full of understanding unlike my first university. They quickly became aware of my past as I felt I could open up to them. Being included in a group of mixed ages, backgrounds, and taking a healthcare qualification, made us all very close. Two of my friends had kids, and we ranged from 30 to Joy and I being the youngest at 20. I had my 21st birthday in December on my first year and so many people came down to my hometown to celebrate. I had: my new OT friends, my university housemates, my NHS friends, my home friends and lots of family surrounding me. I have never felt so loved in my life; it was a perfect night, even if I was a little drunk by the end.

I love to remember this time in my life as "The well year". I know it happened, I know I completed so much in that year, achieved so many things without mental health issues getting in the way. I was not seeing my doctor as much but was still on Risperidone, which seemed to be controlling things. My arms were now only faint scars, and my self-harming had stopped. I had put my demons away, locked them up and thrown away the key.

I successfully and happily completely my first year of Occupational Therapy with a 2.1 pass. I moved home for the summer but had signed up for a house with four girls for my second year. These four girls were my close friends at university, however I am unfortunate not in touch with these friends today. I was excited to move into the house for September 2010, excited to start my second year. Things were finally fitting into place again.

During the summer holiday, two friends and I decided to book a month away travelling to India for August 2010. I had started work back at the hospital, as bank staff for the summer again in the pathology department. Due to changes, I had moved on from being a Medical Lab Assistant to becoming a Phlebotomist. I was able to take blood from patients on the wards and in the outpatients departments, which were then sent to the lab to be analysed. I loved this job and again, got on with everyone there. We had a great laugh and they all wished me well for my adventures to India, knowing I would return to work after.

Travelling was amazing. I had such a brilliant time. My two friends and I didn't stop laughing the whole time, there were no fall out or disagreements, just plain and good old fun. We travelled to Delhi first, a city which I love. Fortunately, I have little sense of smell; it wasn't until our third night that my friends commented on the open urinal we had to walk past each night to get to our hotel. I hadn't even realised this. However, stuff coming from our noses was black, so that was I little give away even if I couldn't smell. We left Delhi and took a 21-day drive around the northern part of India. We visited places like Japipur, Jodhpur, Udaipur and Agra via car and had an amazing local Indian driver. He knew where to take us, and showed us spice shops and local markets on the way. We visited and had our picture taken at the Tar Majal and washed and rode elephants. Our tummies did not exactly agree with the rich Indian food, so we lost a lot of weight but we loved the fresh fruit and smoothes, which were local treats. For our last 10 days, we caught a 48-hour train down south to go on the houseboats in Kelara. We were silently dreading the train, but in fact it was amazing and we had a brilliant time joining in with the locals and making friends. They have a different tradition in India than we do regarding personal property. If you put something down on a table, like an Ipod or book then anyone can pick it up and use it. It was so nice and the locals who we shared our part of the train with loved listening to our music and trying to do our crosswords.

India is an amazing place; I would love to go back. It could be scary, like the time we were followed around because of our skin and hair colour and locals wanted to take pictures with us. We even got on wedding photos. It was a brilliant holiday and I loved it to bits, I'm so pleased I went. However, unfortunately this is where my demons began to sneak up on me again.

It maybe a coincidence but my doctor lowered my Risperidone just before I left for Indian. Like all drugs, this one was having a side effect on my body and increasing the amount of Prolactin I was producing to a dangerous level. So I reduced the amount and that's when things began to change. It was on this holiday, my friend suggested I seek a profession opinion when I arrive back in the UK regarding my moods. I did not recognise there was a major issue at the time, and it didn't effect our holiday. However, recognising the warning signs my friend suggested that something was beginning to happen. Little did they or I know what was going to be in store for the next couple of years.

OCCUPATIONAL THERAPY, THE SECOND YEAR AND THE CHANGE IN MYSELF

As I entered my second year as an Occupational Therapy student at my second University, my life was going to change forever. It was not a dramatic car crash, or an event that I can now look back on and see the change. Instead it was a long winding road into mental illness, as it took control of my body; my life, my heart. It is hard to think back and remember such painful times, but bear with me and join me for the rest of the book as my mental illness takes control.

I suppose things went downhill as soon as I got back from India. Again my memory is very vague at this time and I have a lot of missing pieces with things not quite jig sawing together right. It feels like I am looking back into someone else's life, not my own; not being able to remember bits of my own life. This is a part of the diagnosis I am going to gain on my travels and I will refer to later.

I think it is an important point to make, that as I am remembering or trying to remember these past years I keep being thrown back into that space in time. This makes me disconnect for a while as I relive the memory as if I was there. Sometimes it is pleasant but mostly it is painful. In turn I think this is why some of my memories are blocked out, to keep me safe.

So, returning to September 2010, I had just moved in with my three close friends and another girl. We hit it off well and in fact never argued the whole year. I think you gather so far that I am not an argumentative person and rarely fall out with people. I hate confrontation and will do anything to avoid it. Our house was a mix of all ages, with the youngest a year below me at 20 and the eldest at 28. I felt this meant we got on better as we were all at different stages of our lives. The two friends I went travelling around India with lived with me, plus the other girl who was from my OT course. Everything was happy and we loved sitting watching TV or having Sunday roast together.

The first time I remember there being something really wrong was when the OT course began again in October. We had lived in the house for a couple of weeks and my mood had been up and down gradually getting worse. For some reason on the first day, back I just could not go. This is completely and utterly out of character for me. Even through my rough time in sixth form I had 100% attendance on most terms, so to be left so low that I do not attend classes is a serious issue. I cannot even explain how my mind just would not function to let me out the house to attend university. I sat there crying my eyes out, unable to move, to get dressed or eat. I think this was depression digging its claws in but when you are going though it you just cannot understand why you can't do the things that you love or that make you you. I wanted to go, see my friends, I had left on a good note but I couldn't. Something, some demon was holding me back. This is when my world began to crumple beneath my feet.

Over the next few weeks I became a pile of bones on my bed, crying and being unable to stop the pain that my body was in. My parents and brother picked me up on a regularly basis, either in the day or at night, basically whenever I phoned in heartbreaking tears. It was a 40-minute drive but they must have come at least 3 times a week to take me home, then to bring me back again. I started to visit my local GP at home who put me on some anti-depressants and referred me to the Community mental health team (CMHT). Unfortunately, this was not as straight forward as anyone wished, but he was amazing and used to phone me up nearly every night when I was in away to check I was ok. It took a while for the referral to go through but I was eventually accepted to CMHT and gained another care-coordinator.

I must say at this time, that I know mental health teams get a lot of stick for bad referral times. My parents were struggling with what to do with me and felt helpless, but the local home team gave me their number to ring if I needed them which was amazing as they were in a different catchments CMHT and I was not being referred to them. With that and my GP I think I got amazing care considering the horror stories I have heard.

CMHT aside for one moment, the months leading up to my assessment and referral were not fun. My moods had decided to turn into a fast moving rollercoaster, much more severe than I had experienced before. I went from being unable to move on my bed and totally helpless over things I knew I could do. For example, I had to send off a simple slip for car insurance and I simply could not do it. This was totally unlike me as I love paper work, but again I cannot explain any other way apart from it was all alien to me. My mind and body would not work or function at all. However a completely different person quickly greeted times like these around 5 or 6 days later. I had so much energy you could not shut me up, I mean literally, you could not shut me up. I would talk until my month was dry and sore. I would jump around listen to music and make people dance around with me. I was back to parting all night and having massive spending sprees. Unlike previous experiences, my friends understood and stayed by my side the whole time. I suppose like sixth form they had got to know me as me first and then the demon appeared later. They thought nothing of me trying to climb the outside of the house to fly and instead just took me on walks in the snow and around town to try and calm me down. They took my car keys and bankcard off me to protect me from myself when I was experiencing my most vulnerable highs.

Unfortunately, academic university life was really going downhill too. We had presentations to give and essays to hand in but depending what mood I was in depended what actually happened. I remember two polar opposite occasions when giving presentations in front of our class of around 30. The first was a small group presentation and we had been preparing for a few weeks. On the day I barely pulled myself into university and as I sat there waiting for my turn and listening to others I felt nothing; nothing at all. Not nervousness, not sadness just an empty void. We got up and I went to take my position and to talk my part, got to the front, open my month and nothing came out. Seconds later I burst into hysterical tears and stood there in front of everyone crying. Luckily, my personal tutor was the tutor that day and knew I was struggling so she just sat me down next to herself and gave me a hug. Nothing was mentioned and fortunately it was not an exam. The second presentation I was the complete opposite. Again, it was a group occasion but this time I would not shut up. I was smiling, laughing and talking far too much. My tutor had to take me out of the classroom to calm down. I think everyone was a little confused, as I swung from one reaction to the next happening week by week.

All the tutors at the university were amazing with me throughout my time there, helping me out in all sorts of occasions. I received extensions on essays and extra time to complete mini assignments. They could all tell that something was wrong but kept treating me as an equal although helping me get through it on a personal level. My personal tutor was amazing and I still occasionally see her to this day. I remember sitting and crying with her on many occasions when things had got too much. She often helped me to arrange to see my care coordinator when things were to severe for her to handle. She was again my lifeline at university and I believe we got rather close.

One thing that makes me proud and happy to this day is I was able to complete my second year at university, apart from the placement. I was on one hell of a ride but I completed all my assignments, passing them all and even getting a 1st on two modules. I also still stayed within my friendship group and manage to have some good times. Although I had a hard time coping some of the time, the times I didn't I was out with everyone having a laugh and still being that fun loving girl that they once knew. I remember having my 22nd birthday and going pot painting for the day. I always loved my birthday, but this was the hardest day ever. I spent the morning crying but my friend picked me up and took me pot painting for the afternoon. It was brilliant and i had a great time, I think everyone did. Times like this are special for me to remember, as although I know I was hurting for the day it is like seeing the sun breaking though the clouds if only for a short period.

My friends never let me down through anything at university. Chloe, my closest friend there used to sit and look after me time after time. She came with me to my first couple of CMHT appointments and helped me connect with my new care coordinator. She was amazing and a friend that literally kept me alive again. She would sit with me as I cried uncontrollable, ringing the crisis team or my parents for help, she would always keep her cool and never judged me.

My disconnecting, semi-conscious episodes and self-harming behaviours had re-entered my life at this stage and began to take control again. I devastatingly remember my first cut on the clean arms that were to never look the same again. I was sat on the floor of my bedroom, with my pills all out of their boxes, out on show. I wondered whether to take a overdose to kill myself or to temporarily control the pain by cutting myself. Both seemed viable options at the time, both with unpleasant repercussions. I was now on a health course so I knew that to self-harm again would be disastrous, but in the end the pain was too much. I cut. I felt that rush and was hooked. I could not hide it for long, and it quickly became my coping strategy again. Eight years on from that first cut, my self-harm got out of control and caused unthinkable damage. However, as for the pills or the cutting, I think I chose the right way.

Life was still difficult at university. I was barely making it to class and if I did I had episodes of disconnection and couldn't remember things from the day. How I manage to stay there and how I kept going I will never know. I think I have the strength of one hundred men inside me that keeps me going though anything. Unfortunately, placement was one thing too many.

Placement was due to start in January 2011; I had been given a hand therapy placement, that if I was well would of been a very exciting six weeks. Unfortunately, occupational health would not pass me to go on the placement and I had to withdraw and postpone it to the summer. This did not bother me too much, as I believed I would be well by the summer and definitely be able to complete it then. Regrettably, as I found out, mental illness does not work like that. I stayed at my university house most of the time when the others were on placement. I liked having the time to myself and was able to do the cleaning and cooking for everyone. I also began to get back equated with my secret life, the mental health appointment lifestyle.

My CMHT team was ok, and I started my seeing my care coordinator Ann weekly. She and I would talk through what was going on and try to come up with plans to help me get through the week. The psychiatrist quickly saw me and me a prescribed mood stabiliser, Carbamazepine, as well as my Risperidone and mirtazapine an anti-depressant. At first these seemed to stabilise my mood to a children's rollercoaster. I think this is what helped me complete my second year academically. Consequently, this is also when I found writing to be an external outlet of my feelings. Staff and friends were finding it hard to deal with my mood changes so to help them out I started to explain them as the weather.

WEATHER CHANGES

At all times I am a live for the moment girl and have always disliked reflecting on any of my troubles, symptoms or past, until I found writing. In fact, I avoid dwelling on anything at all; I like to and am very good at boxing things away and laughing everything off. To be honest, even on short reflection I think it's a good survival technique, although it seems to have got me in some bother. I always forget my bad days and my high days and instead live on the days that I am stable, remembering them as MY life.

As said, I live for the moment, when I am well I live day by day. So to reflect on my past or indeed my future is hard. When I first saw the psychiatrist I was asked to complete mood charts over several months to determine my mood fluctuations. I found this hard as I was not aware of any patterns and didn't like to refer everything to mood. I felt like I was clicking into different states or 'moods' very quickly because when you're living the change they seem so quick, however writing it down I could see when the clouds start forming and when sunshine starts to rise. Describing my moods by weather seems the best way to replicate what my life actually held.

THE CLOUDS

Clouds seem to form one day, seemly from nowhere, pushed over from some forgotten land. They slowly start appearing over your head like a mist of the brain making everything so hard and exhausting. For a few days you hold on, on to hope, on to being brave. You get through the day by using what other people would describe as the minimal amount of effort but for you is using the energy of your entire body. But the clouds keep coming, forming thick and fast smothering you whole until everything gets so dark. Pitch black. The darkness comes so fast that you can barely see or hear yourself anymore. Becoming trapped, you result in a pile on your bed scared to move or to feel. As for now you only exist as a heartbeat and a quite breath. Your voice stops, time disappears and the only relief you can find is to sleep. Hours, days or weeks can go by in this state of un-existence until the clouds begin to move. If you're unfortunate, with their move arises a great pain from within. Like a death plenty has come over your body and you are willing to do anything for an escape. Unable to breathe, tears roll down your face as you are focused on the floor clutching at your body at it shakes. Then you are left with chanting death plans and huge pain covering your entire body. For some time you can be trapped in this state, until the clouds start to move ever so slowly and you can hear your voice and thoughts coming back alive. You can feel your soul re enter your body and your energy levels rising. But sometimes, if you are lucky the clouds can clear quickly, as if by magic. You suddenly don't feel that pull on your body that is dragging you down and the concept of thinking is not a strange phenomenon anymore. This hell has come to an end and the time is then forgotten. Boxed away; out of sight, out of mind as they say. Not daring to dwell on the days you lost your soul, you move on. A new day: A new you.

THE SUNSHINE

Sunshine comes just like the weather. It brings smile and laughter and a chance to play outside. It builds up inside you, like your soul jumping around wanting to get out, want to do so much, to do everything. Everything that you wanted to do, you can do it. All your childhood dreams can come true. There is no stopping you now, you have the power. You are beautiful. The doubt and low self worth goes, you are you, you are better than you, you are the best, you are the Queen. 'Voices' tell you how great life is, how fun life is, how exciting life can be. You are a genius, a master of all, a someone that everyone should know! Taking on every talent that you have you feed the jumping soul. You talk and talk and talk some more until all the brilliant ideas can't even fit into your month. So you scribble everything down, write publishable poetry and draw saleable pictures, creating magnificent pieces of art. Everything seems to connect to you in a magical way. Music fills your body pulsing with every beat of your heart. Food tastes like it's never tasted before, you can feel every texture and all senses tingle with excitement. Until you cannot stop: No really you can't stop. You realise you haven't stopped moving for days, you haven't slept and your brain hasn't had any rest. The jiggling soul starts to hurt but you can't control it. People start to irriate you, everyone is doing things so slow you have to bite your tongue to not scream and shout. You try sitting still, but your heads feel like it has pins and needles of the brain. Then it comes – your chance. If only for a brief second, that glimpse of mellowing settling in the distance. You have to set free the beast inside you. Calm yourself; take steps to return to the smooth party of life. Everything still bright, light and happy but the sun is slowly going down. You can feel it in your bones, in your spine, in your heart. Things are settling and life is back to a mellow party. A party you want to be a part of. You now have pain free productivity with more than enough energy to last the day but to leave rested and silent at night. The jiggling soul is boxed away but you feel you can go like this forever.

THE PEACE

When the dust settles down and you return from your rollercoaster of weather there is peace. The hours, days and weeks are packed away into boxes only to be opened for line of comedy with your friends. It's good, you are you, you're back. You like being just you, to function at a normal speed. To finish off deadlines, go to meetings and be settled in your own skin. But you're on edge, there is one problem –What weather is around the next corner??

Using the weather to explain my moods became extremely handy for any situation to explain what I was going through. Knowing that I could now explain what was happening in my life though writing gave me a new sense control and power. Once I got settled on my medication my moods started to settle down I began opening up to Ann about my disconnecting episode and loosing time. I did not know them as separate symptoms at the time, and though there were just another product of my moods. Below is a letter that I wrote to Ann that got me in touch with Henry, a psychiatrist of psychotherapy who specialises in personality disorders.

LETTER TO ANN, 2011, BIG SECRET RELEASED

Dear Ann,

I wrote this after our meeting and think it is time I need to share...

Today, Friday 4th March 2011, I have just come back from a meeting with yourself. The meeting went fine, however afterwards I became very upset. I don't seem to be able to explain or tell you anything that I really want to. Often I come home and cry to Chloe or my dad spilling out things that sometimes I didn't even know I was thinking. At the most recent meeting, it was initially going quite well, I had had a good week and my moods seem to be settling down. However, I think I started to become unsettled when I asked you if I had a diagnosis or not. You explained that we would ask the Doctor at our next appointment and that it may be some type of mood disorder, which I can understand, but you also said about my past history.

For some reason this really upset me. When I went back to Chloe I was hysterical and I couldn't explain why this had upset me so much... (maybe because I just want it over and then for someone to remove it for good!)... But all this stuff came out...I feel I need to explain what has been happing since the beginning. I have never felt comfortable explaining this about myself to anyone and have gone along with what 'people' say and how I SHOULD feel (This is mainly with EIT care-co)... So as it seems that I cannot talk about things, I thought I would try writing it down. (I hope that's ok!)

Everything starts from the fact that I believe that there is more than one person living inside me. Not in a psychotic way, I mean I know that

there is not actually two people inside, but there is 2 people alive. There is me Milly and then there is something, someone else: Someone that is core inside my body. They come out at various points in the day/week/month. They overrun my body thinking things that I wouldn't think, acting in ways that I wouldn't act. Knowing this, and saying that someone else is telling me to do things is why I think EIS thought I was psychotic at first. I do hear voices from the outside of my body...however I also experience them inside and they are the bad person/thing. This someone is deep inside me, at the core, but it's not me, I CAN'T controlled it! It appears and takes control of my: actions, emotions, body, both in a depressed way, in a happy/buzzing way and a disconnected way. This is what was happening last time. I got put on Risperidone and it worked, but I also left university, moved home, had a break.

So the environmental factors also helped my mood stabilise- well, be controllable. But this thing has never gone. I want it REMOVED. I don't know how to explain. My moods ARE my problems and over the past few months they have been uncontrollable, but IS IT the person inside me that is controlling them? I have had stable points in my life when my mood isn't so extreme, so controlling, but it is always there, this separate person, is it creating this mood aura. I have shown my mood symptoms and how they are affecting my life at the moment, and I do feel/hope that the medication is actually starting to help. My moods are becoming less frequently changing, and the person is coming alive less often... But will they ever go?? Is it normal?? How do I control them??

I hate it as much as it hates me, but recently it has been winning and I am having to deal with the scars and emotional impact it's leaving on my body and my friends. Milly is the one who has to explain it to people, but how can I when I don't even know what it is?

I hope this doesn't sound nuts, because I am not meaning it in a nuts way and I am not nuts. I just don't think anyone has understood me so far, people have picked up the wrong end of the stick (Not so much this time and with trying to help the mood swings, but EIT DID) and I am really scared of being abandoned like last time, because I don't know how much more of it I can take.

I hope this makes some sense, as it is still confusing for me too, but it has been buried for far too long. I feel I am ready to start talking about things and will do anything to get this thing out of me so that I don't make a mistake that is irreversible. Sorry if this has annoyed you by writing it down, but I need to start living instead of constantly looking over my shoulder and I don't know how else to get it away.

I hoping you understand, and you can help
Thank you
Milly Jones

IN THAT MOMENT

At the time of writing this letter I was so confused but needed to get out how I felt. I believed that I had 2 people inside me for a very long time but do not hold this belief anymore as I have a greater understanding of myself. I had no idea what was going on, but the letter assisted me in getting the right help.

Unfortunately, summer came and I was unable to go on placement again. The hardest thing I had to do that year was hand in the piece of paper saying that I was having to take a year out. I remember sitting there in front of the course leader crying my eyes out and getting a big hug. Everyone was so supportive and I got such nice emails from a couple of staff saying how strong I was and that I would pull through. Deep down though, I felt like a failure again, and was a mess for a few weeks after. Looking back now, I cannot really remember that time, protected by blacking it all out unconsciously. However, I soon realised I had a greater support system in place than I did have before.

I sent the Letter to Ann off in March and began seeing Henry for an assessment period in June 2011. I had left my university course in May and moved out the same month. It was decided that I should stay under the care of my university town's CMHT as it was hoped by everyone that I would be returning to university within the next year. I was very pleased with the situation, as I dislike change and was close to Ann. Plus I felt things were finally moving forward and I was getting the right help to get me onto that shiny road of recovery. Hindsight though is a marvelous thing, and having to travel to and from university so much was not a brilliant idea.

SNIPPET INTO MY MIND - THOUGHTS – INTRUSIVE, REPARATIVE AND IMPLANTED

The truth. I've always been told to tell the truth. Everyone is always told to tell the truth from being little. But what do you do when you don't know what the truth is anymore? What do you do when you don't know how you feel, that you can't believe the thoughts in your head. That the thoughts in your head aren't even always your own, they do not appear from within. There can be intrusive thoughts, or repetitive thoughts, thoughts that have been implanted into you head. You do not own these thoughts, why are they even here?

So you try your best to be honest to yourself and everyone around you but you just can't believe what things are actually running though your head. The whole of your life you feel like a fake because what you say and what you do can be different to what the thoughts that swill around in your conscious mind.

Intrusive thoughts come out of the darkness and hit you like a ton of bricks. They say things like – pull out on that guy, push her over the bridge. Or bring images up of upsetting scenes and unpleasant situations. There is no control over what you hear from that though, it is not yours, you cannot stop it. You can try to argue back but by the time you have realised the thought even existed it has gone, and you have to move on. You cannot dwell on the past.

Repetitive thoughts are thoughts, which are on a link in your brain; these may last for hours, days and sometimes weeks. You cannot get the same line or rhyme out of your head and there is no control over the thought. It is a bit like having a song stuck in your head, however you can think over the repetitive thoughts whilst they still chant away. You cannot stop them from happening and they are on a continuous loop, a never-ending cycle. My recent one was 'As I sit cocooned on my bed, the devil has decided to dance in my head'. This was a line from one of my poems but I could not get it away for just over a week. It drove me mad. Lines can get stuck in, seemingly from anywhere, they can start off as a normal thought, but then that thought seems to go into over drive.

Implanted thoughts are much like intrusive thoughts, however you believe you have thought them. You can be trapped for days or weeks thinking paranoid ideas or thoughts of unsettling things. It is only when you are released from the hands of the implanting beast that you realise you were not thinking clearly and these were not your thoughts. Unlike intrusive thought, they do not disappear quickly and you do have time to analyse them after they have gone. Although, you may act a little crazy for a while whilst they are around

Really this just touches on some of the different thoughts that can occur within our minds. I know that there are many more, however these are my main ones, which I battled with everyday in sixth form and until now. But these thoughts are different to voices. Having different inner voices in your head is like having different people. These voices sound like your reading voice but multiple, making you feel there are different people inside you. So I have multiple thought processes and multiple voices but are they a part of me or a symptom? If I didn't have these types of thoughts, or voices I would feel a little bit odd! In the end I wouldn't be me.

But how do I separate me from what professionals want to hear. If I have lived with the voices and thoughts all my life how do I know they are not normal?

THERAPY

I began psychotherapy in September 2011 after a few assessment sessions with Henry. I was still under a psychiatrist who I saw every 6 months and was stable (ish) on my combination of Risperidone, Mirtazapine and Carbamazepine. My moods were settling down but they seemed to have left a huge whole and difficulties in my psychological self. The letter I wrote was discussed at a CPA by Ann, Henry and my psychiatrist, which resulted in an assessment period with Henry. I was then, quickly placed under a psychiatrist who was in training to become a psychotherapist and began seeing him weekly for 9 months.

In the year leading up to my therapy, I had been under and seen by a counsellor and a CBT therapist at the university who had both explained that I was too ill and needed a more professional help. This made me nervous of accepting a therapeutic process again and as deep down I knew there maybe something more to address.

Henry and my therapist were particularly interested in the times that I disconnected and became semi-conscious. They diagnosed these episodes as periods of dissociation. I had never heard this term at the time but when he explained it to me it made complete sense. Everyone dissociated sometimes, I just did it to the extreme. Have you ever driven to work one morning, on a route that you know so well so that when you arrive you cannot remember the drive. Well that is dissociation, or finding you have a brew next to you that you can't remember making or drinking. Again, I do this to the extreme. For example I can come round in an unfamiliar place, not knowing how I got there. Or I could wake up one morning with a bandage on my arm unsure of what is underneath. Things were finally making sense.

Dissociating now dates back to my sixth form years and the time I had 'panic attacks' which were not they. It is scary to think back!

Looking back I think I was in the completely wrong period in my life to be completing therapy. I was travelling to and fro to university to have intense therapy sessions, which would often leave me dissociating and a danger to others and myself. I ended up in A&E multiple times after therapy and felt it was doing more harm than good.

I often did not last the whole hour of the session and found them too much to handle. In fact on one particularly bad day, I only lasted 20 minutes and then drove home hitting and killing a bird on the way. I dissociated at the time but can remember coming round in a place I did not know with tears streaming down my face. I knew I had hit a bird but after that I am not sure. Not only was the therapy wrong for me, it was dangerous. I could not recognise this at the time and continue going, thinking, believing, hoping it would help.

Looking back now, discussing this period in time with Kate, I feel I was not in the right place for therapy. Kate explains it to me; it was if they had said and concluded that I was ill and then rushed into therapy. They did not give me coping strategies to handle the can of worms in which they were opening, in turn creating a therapy process that did not work. Only having experience this do I now understand when people say you are too ill for therapy. If you cannot cope, you shut down and there is no point to doing it: as I found out.

I was given the diagnosis of Multiple Personality Disorder in January 2012; now known as a Dissociate Disorder. The therapist would ask me who I was today and built ideas in my head. I felt I was unable to process what was happening or what I actually thought. I had to go along with what they were saying. It was like they want you to admit a deep dark secret, even if you did not know one. I didn't find therapy helpful in the end, and feel I was pressured into it. I did not accept my diagnosis, as it was never explained to me. I remember my last session with my therapist saying 'Thank you, I have learnt a lot from you'. I feel that just sums it up really, he learnt a lot from me and I was more confused than ever.

ONE LIFE ENDS AND ANOTHER BEGINS

Life moving away from my old university town was a lot harder than moving after my life at my first university town. I had created a new life, new brilliant friends, independence and a career path. I thought everything was fitting into place and I was happy until everything blew up. My mental illness, here my known as my demons, took all at this away from me. As l was forced to leave my new home behind, and move back to parents, a sense of grieving came over my body.

I tried my best to stay close with my new friends. I did not want to leave this university town or my life behind so it took me weeks to settle down and into a new routine. I decided to defer for the year, taking a year out to get well and rid of my demons. I believed a year would be more then long enough to get better, and then I could carry on like normal. Last time it seemed like a holiday worked to get me sorted, but this was not going to be the case. Although close with my friends at university, as they moved into their third year we began to drift apart. Their lives became so different to mine and things were beginning to change. I thought, hoped and crossed my heart that this wouldn't happen. But fighting to try and regain my old life whilst battling my demons is near enough impossible. I was becoming a service user instead of a professional. The lines with my friends became crossed, as I was no longer seen as a student, which is how we made friends in the first place. We began to have less and less in common and our lives separated down different paths. Although we did not fall out and I still speak to one or two from University occasionally, I could not hold on to my old life.

When I moved away from university in May, I was still committed to visiting nearly twice every week within the next year. I had appointments with Ann, Henry, Psychiatrists, one to one therapy and group therapy. In this mix I tried to see my friends as much as possible, trying ignoring the jealousy I felt at their lives. However, little did I know I was about to make a new set of friends who understood me completely entering an entirely different life.

In October 2011 I began a fortnightly group session, on a Tuesday morning. It was a rolling Psychology Educational group formed to educate service users with a variety of demons around mental health. The content included: self-harm, negative thinking, personality development, treatment and recovery. Some of the sessions worked well for others and I, but some did not. For example, we had two sessions on self-harm and were asked various ways in which you could self-harm. Being a group of people who have acqired this as a coping strategy we quickly came up with a list of ways that are considered harmful to ourselves. In the end we had three A3 pieces of paper up on the wall listing many self-harming ways. To us this seemed more like a tip sharing session then actually helping us. To this day we look back and giggle at the gathering because it was conducted totally wrong and clearly not thought out that well. This was a main indicator I definitely was now a service user as well as training professional.

The best part of the psychology education group was the friendship group which had formed. We had more fun and learnt more outside the sessions than in the dedicated time. We quickly became friends and met up after the sessions, going for coffee or dinner at a local cafe. I felt this made my travel to therapy more worthwhile as I was creating a new set of friends. In turn this meant I was not relying on my university friends to be around when I went up. It was hard driving there and back if there was not a nice reason to go; if it was all going to be down to my demons.

In January 2012 the group changed and there were only three of the original members left, myself included. However, again we bonded quickly and I am still in touch with these friends to this day. From the first group I met one of my closest friends, a person I truly believe will never not be in my life From the first group I met one of my closest friends, a person I truly believe will never not be in my life. Beth is an amazing person and has had to live with so much, but we can relate to together through our demons.

We have only met each other a handful of times but text every single day without fail. She was also a university student but had to defer for the year. She lived near me, so like me, travelled a lot to keep under the care of the CMHT in this university town. It's been nearly three years since she first sat next me in that group with the opening line 'yeah, someone who is young'. I was so shy at the beginning that I haven't opened my mouth for the first two sessions but with this smiling face looking at me; I had to talk back. As we spoke, I could see the demon in her that I knew so well, that smile on her face, tear in her eye, the mask she was hiding behind. These quickly became our connection, and we understood each other in a new language quickly became our connection, and we understood each other in a new language. Beth moved back home in the summer of 2012 and then lived in London for a year. We have always been at least a two-hour drive from each other, but I feel she knows me better then I know myself. We text each other every day despite our struggles or ringing each other up in tears. Together we understand and do not judge for our connection is strong.

Beth was not part of the second group as she was forced to enter another type of therapy. Two men and I carried on and a lady and another young girl joined us. Out of the pain, we all quickly became good friends and the young girl quickly became of my good friends. Unfortunately, we have a deep connection that I wish no one had has she is a smart girl with terrible mental health issues. We have extremely similar symptoms but have been treated completely different. The first thing I remember about meeting her was her attending the first and second session in a wheel chair, unable to walk or move her legs. We didn't think anything of this or judge assuming she was physically disabled. However, on the third session she came in her chair and ended up sitting near the door. Disliking this position, she suddenly got up and walked across the room, extremely wobbly and holding on to chairs but walking none the less. We all looked shocked and rather bewildered. As the weeks counted by, the young girl came in on crutches the week after and then a few weeks later appeared with only one crutch and walking well. It was like a miracle, going from her being unable to move her legs to walking. She eventually explained how she had conversion disorder, which is were emotional pain is turned psychical. She has been paralysed for six months and then had to learn to walk again, all because of her mental health.

We still look back on this day and how funny it was, suddenly walking across the room. It is a serious matter but something we laugh and joke about to get through.

At the time I had not heard of such disorder but for a couple of years it affected my life. One year on I was also diagnosed with Conversion disorder, which is one reason why Lucy and I are so similar in nature. My current care coordinator Kate jokes that when there are miracle cures in America at these conferences that maybe they all have conversion disorder. Conversion disorder will be explained fully later on but is defined as turning emotional pain physical like Lucy explained to us.

All these friends that I met at these groups were, and still are amazing. I see and speak to Lucy a couple of times a week but unfortunately she still lives in nearly a hour away but thanks to technology we are still close. With everyone else from these groups, we know we are there for each other no matter what. We text occasionally and meet up for meals but I know if I have a problem they will be there, straight by my side.

Crazy friendships are a different friendship to others through a mutual understanding of pain and demons. I love these friends dearly and wrote a poem to express what they mean.

To My Crazy Friends

Craziness can appear in any situation
No need for schedule
No need for occasion

Demons can happen at any point
Regardless of invitation
Regardless of blood

Through acceptance of life I am starting to discover
People with my way of thinking
People battling to recover

I count myself lucky that I have been able to find
A new kind of friendship
A new way to survive

Our closeness was designed whilst tangled in a web
Something we never created
Something we sadly dread

But fighting through rain and calming down the sun
We have become connected
We have become as one

This is to you, the friend I have made
Linked together by trust
Linked together by trade

Our friendship is connected on a whole different level
Understanding of appointment
Understanding of the devil

Somehow we are able to laugh about our lives
Making our times enjoyable
Making us able to survive

We are all connected through our own special language
Words can be dissimilar
Words can be silent

Even though it is diverse this land that we all share
Connections are emotional
Connections are there

Collectively we discuss all the fears in our heads
Our trust is invincible
Our trust is never dead

Milly Jones

Although it is sad that we were united by the weather
Our connection will last
Our connection will be forever

I would not be here without the heart of my friends
Hold hands though the sun
Hold hands though the rain

I guess this is a poem in which I am trying to say
Thank you for being you
Thank you for not going away

LIFE CARRIED ON

Travelling for therapy and seeing Ann and my friends became hard and time consuming. I was hoping that I was getting better but things were just getting more and more intense and my head became an utter mess. Determination inside, I carried on through. I was determined to get back into Occupational Therapy and complete my placement believing that would be the best way would be to keep learning and to get a job.

In 2011 when I initially put my Occupational Therapy course on hold I signed up for and am still completing a CBT course, Level 5, with an online provider. I love to study and academically minded so this was something to keep myself occupied. I also started applying for part time jobs and in May 2012 I had a successful interview for a care worker job for a local provider. This was going to include, visiting people's homes, giving out medication and help with self-care. I was very excited to start working again, thinking it would lead me on to the right track to recovery. My moods had stabled out and I thought I was keeping all the craziness of my falling apart in my psychological self to one side. This however, as I was to find out is impossible.

In August 2011 I started my training to be a healthcare assistant. It had taken a while for all the paper work and CRB clearing to come through, but I was excited none the less. The training was a 45 minutes drive away and I was late on the first day after being given the wrong place to meet. With the adrenaline running this did not bother me and I walked in confidently and quickly became friends with the three other people on our course. The first day went well, we studied epilepsy and took a short exam on different types of medication. I was enjoying my time there, feeling included as a member of society where no one knew the pain or difficulties I was in. I felt a part of life again and was looking forward to returning on the second day.

The next morning came and I felt normal as I arose. I got to the centre early this time and managed to grab a brew before the start. On that day we learnt hoisting and got to have a go lifting people up and pushing them around. We then had dinner and spent our time giggling at some television programme from the night before. Again, we had an exam on what we had learnt so that we could get a certificate and be able to use the hoist on our own with clients. However, this is where my life went wrong, yet again.

I remember sitting there, looking at a power point presentation on the wall and suddenly it all started to dance around and go blurry. I felt hot and faint and really unwell. I stumbled out of the room and can't really remember much more. Next thing I know there were three paramedics around me asking me to raise my arms. I did, well I thought I did, but I was unable to raises my left arm. I was taken to the back of the ambulance and had an ECG and observations done on me. I was starting to come round at this point but kept getting blurry eyes and would disconnect for a while. The paramedics took me off to hospital where I was admitted for the night.

It was an altogether scary experience. Like anyone in that situation, I thought I was having a stroke, or some type of MS attack. I had various neurology exams that showed a weakness to my left side but apparently no brain damage. I just spent one night in hospital and was discharger late the next day. I was sent for an MRI the day after and then did not really hear much for a few weeks. On my discharge letter it was queried that I had had a hemiplegic migraine attack. This was unexplained to me but when I looked it up back at home, it seemed to make sense.

I visited my local amazing GP and he reassured me and helped push through the follow up appointment to neurology. I was put on some new medication for blood pressure, which are showed to reduce migraine attacks. Whilst growing up I had daily headaches and was under neurology investigation for a couple years. My GP explained that this could be linked so the diagnosis fit even more.

I was eventually seen by a neurologist in November 2012. The initial appointment seemed to be going well and she understood where I was coming from. That was until I apparently slapped her in the face. I do not mean literally mind, I only showed her my arms. My now very scarred and silently cut arms. It was as if I had started to beat her up. Her reaction completely changed and so did the atmosphere in the room. The appointment was soon over and I was quick to leave. My mum was surprised at such reactions at a symptom of a mental illness; regrettably I was not. Mental health sometime gets this reaction and I was used to it. The neurologist did however refer me for an EEG and showed me that my MRI was clean. Unfortunately, I could not cope with her reaction so changed neurologist to visit the same Doctor who I saw when I was sixteen with my headaches.

Snippet in my mind - Believe in yourself poem

To look at me, I may seem well.
But there is a side I do not tell.
Wrapped in barbed wire on the outside
I am contently fighting to stay alive.

But it is now as I sit cocooned on my bed
That the devils have decided to dance in my head,
Their tears bruised my eyes and beat up my soul.
They think and plan and take control.

They do not care what harm they cause.
Bulling and hacking away at my flaws
They destroy the me that wants to live
Creating a part that has had to be hid

I do not recognize the self I have made
The one who is cowering and become afraid
I cannot understand who this creature is I see
I'm scared to look around in case it is me

For I can no longer see what is inside
But I know there's a girl who was once alive
Hiding under the words which cannot be said
She is buried down deep I'm convinced she is dead

That little frightened girl is loved by so many
She strong, thoughtful and above all caring
Her bubbly personality guarantees a smile
And her laugh is contagious because it's a cackle

Her determination is unique
Some say it should be bottled
A creative mind brings out the best in her
And should never be forgotten

But where is this girl when I open my eyes
Why is she cocooned?
Why does she hide?

For this is me that I cannot see
That little light that needs to be free
I cannot recognise this me no more
The one I've forgotten the one I've engorged

I see evil
I see pain,
I don't see what they describe

I see someone who does not deserve
To breathe
To move
To be alive

But when will I open
Open my eyes
To recognises this me inside

I need her to grow
To show her face
To take away all this anger and hate.

Although I cannot see this me no more
She has gone into hiding but I must not engorge

If I continue to run and hate
And build up things that cannot be said
This little me that's started to hide
May disappear completely one night

I need to trust
I need to share
I need to understand that people are there

It will take time
It will take hope
But baby steps will help the most.

So this is to you
A poem to yourself
Believe in that little you
And become a success!

DETERMINATION

Although I had all this going on: neurology appointments, group therapy, one to one therapy and seeing Ann, I did not give in. I was now battling with: episodes where my left side would be weakened for weeks at a time, stages of dissociation, mood swings, self harm, inside and outside voices attacking my self perception of thoughts that were around the multiple people inside me. I was still not connecting any of them together and thought of my life as separate parts. However I did not give in and started to accept my mental illness as me, all be it multiple people.

Finding my legs became a new way to express my self-harm so I decided to go back to phlebotomy at my local hospital in November 2012. I loved this job and it only seems like a couple of months since I was practicing, but in fact it was nearly two years since I stopped. Going back was no different to being off for the weekends. Nothing had changed, everyone was still so friendly and inviting and the job was brilliant. I thoroughly loved my time at work. But unfortunately, like everything in my life and with everything going on, something had to snap. And it was I, yet again.

Just before Christmas 2012 I ended up in A&E having self harmed pretty badly. I needed stitching and it was right across my arm meaning I would be unable to work at the hospital. Luckily, my boss knew my background, as I had had several unresponsive moments whilst working for her. Plus everyone had seen my scarred arms! She was surprised but supportive and due to circumstances I had to leave this job for while. I am still bank staff so can go back when well enough, but unfortunately five years on and I am still not in the right place.

Self-harm poem

I self harmed again tonight,
I not overly sure why,
My mind took control of me,
I cannot tell a lie.

I do not do it for attention,
I do not do it for blood
Somehow I ended up A&E again
But luckily I was not judged

It a funny thing this self harming lark
All of us don't seem to know why
We can't understand how you cutting yourself
Can make you feel so alive

For me I am different
I am not always the same
I go through stages of normality
Which is then broken by the pain

So sometimes I crack
Maybe for a few weeks
I turn in the unbearable pain physical
As I take control in a flip

It may be unhealthy
It will be grim,
I may need emergency help
But you can judge from within

For a minute in time I have control
I am starting to understand why
Creating my own pain for once
Unfortunately builds a mini high

When things are as unstable as all this
Pain regains control
I can finally grab some power over myself
But regrettably it shows

This is the coping strategy I have learnt
Developing from a child
I do not enjoy doing this to myself
Fortunately am starting to see why

THE CHANGE

Although I couldn't see it at the time, opportunely Ann, my care coordinator fell pregnant and Henry was retiring so I was transferred to my home CMHT in August 2012. I was now enjoying living at home the best I could but was devastated as to the fact that I was being transferred; worried that the CMHT would reject me. The transfer between other teams was messy and the referral into my university CMHT was difficult. I would like to say this transfer was smooth sailing, but it wasn't. It was recommended by Henry that I was to have 6 months off therapy before beginning something new. I felt as if I was going from all this care and twice weekly appointments to nothing. What really hurt though was I felt I was losing my connection with my university town. The town that was supposed to move my life on: the town I was supposed to become a professional in. My demons had now taken this away and I did not want my new friends to go as well.

SNIPPET OF MY MIND -
PICK YOURSELF UP AND
BRUSH YOURSELF OFF

I was not under any care for the period of August to November 2012 and this piece was written as my determination carries on. I felt I needed to explain my past to people and indeed my future choice, as I was to take my Seventh degree course. I love and hate that I have started so many degrees, but it shows strength and determination in life. Something that I feel need to be encouraged by everyone and to everyone.

I think I have learnt that in life that you have to keep going, pick yourself back up and try again, whatever life throws at you. Having my weather changes, psychotic symptoms and dissociative episodes brings the inevitable fact that I will keep becoming ill throughout life. But the does not mean I will not part take in life anymore. I now believe it is how you cope after the storm, after the conditions have taken hold which counts.

My life has been anything but smooth sailing since I got my first bout of depression and psychosis in 2007, at the age of 17. As said earlier, I was admitted to a mental health hospital for a few weeks by the early intervention team and shortly, after being released, sent off to my first university. This was the first incident of my motto of 'pick yourself up and push yourself off'. It wasn't the brightest of ideas, escaping to University, but it wasn't the worst either. Looking back I do not regret it and have learnt a lot about myself in those years.

Unfortunately my rocky road began in those young years of becoming a teenager. Although throughout the years I have started getting my life back on track, with help of medication and support of my family. I moved between university worlds and jobs and lived most my life back at home. I become 'well' for just over 2 years in 2008 to 2010 where I held down a job, a social life, and managed a move to a new University. I created great new friends and was able to travel around India! But then something clicked again and my life began to change. Unknowingly and quite unexpectedly I applied my motto again. As I left my second university, leaving friends and my degree behind, I picked myself and brushed myself off.

I have been through therapy which attacked the rigid hold on myself and taught me to accept all of me but I am contently moulding myself to my new life and I still need a lot of help. I have been unable to work due to mental health problem but will not give in. Trying to be a health care assistant, trying to go back to phelbotomany only to be knocked down by my demons. To other it may look as laughable times of madness, or periods of sadness but these are moments that can cause a lot of upset. I believe this should be a life worth living, not a life hanging on terrified what condition is around the next corner. So I am battling through again. I am still unable to work because I am still unstable but I have started my 7th university course and have opted for an Open University degree. It's very laughable that it is my 7th degree course, but to be honest I'm proud. I am proud that I have kept going every time. I have pulled myself up, brushed myself off and carried on.

My life has been so different to all of my friends. I have seen my high school friends all graduate, grow up and become independent adults. I have then seen my second University friends also go ahead and graduate get qualified jobs whilst I was left behind. But my path now leads me to graduate in 3 years time and I am determined not to give up and let this mental illness win (fingers crossed that the sun doesn't makes me start an 8th Uni course)

To others my path in life may seem broken, but there is a reason behind every story and mental illness is mine. I know that a purpose in life can go along way even if that is just doing 4 hours of study a week. Although my course in occupational therapy was amazing, I was unable to complete it. I think it has worked as therapy though, to ensure I keep an occupation in my life. I maybe on a different track to all my friends and the 'right way' for society but I am trying my best and keeping going even when it's easier to give up. Life is never plain sailing and I suppose you have to make the most of what you have got! So pick yourselves up, brush yourselves off and carry on.

CCTT (Complete Care and Treatment Team) team eventually accepted me in December 2012. The following year I changed a lot, but my determination never left.

TRANSFER AND NEW LIFE

I started seeing Kate, my new care-coordinator with the CCTT in November 2012. Sorry to say, but I didn't feel we bonded initially and it was hard to get over what was happening in my life. Kate was a really nice person and so easy to get on with, but I felt it was my personal problem why we first did not initially bond. I was so nervous and so unsure what she had gleamed from the other CMHT team that I placed a barrier between us. I hated the building as a place; I found it difficult to attend, as it was where I had been snatched into hospital years before.

Luckily, nearly two years later I became rather close to Kate and she literally became my lifeline. She can have me admitting anything, crying one minute and laughing the next. She was so human; this will be covered later, as she was amazing.

I had had three months away from therapy and away from help when the referral was finally though. Within this time I had relapsed in my moods badly. It was as though the Carbamazepine had stopped working as well as it should. I had been given an increase by my GP and was now on a very high dose, though it seemed to be helping very little. The best and only way to explain my mood rollercoaster is to take you on it.

DEPRESSION

A lot people unfortunately experience depression, it is something I would not wish on my worst enemy. I question a lot about what I feel and whether other people feel it too. It is strange to thinking that some people have never felt the pain of depression and it is as alien to them as it is for someone who has felt it not to have experienced it. Personally, I think there are stages of depression, starting with the demons inside, and the gathering clouds.

<u>DO YOU EVER?</u>

Do you ever think that your soul is bad for this world, that it doesn't belong?

That there is chronic feeling of ghosts surrounding your body and you are becoming to have an altered mind?

That these ghosts will never leave you alone, no matter what you are doing, even if you become happy about life. They are always there, within your body.

Do you start to pray every night that when you close your eyes it will be for the last time and don't want to get up?

<u>Stage one, Depression.</u>

Do you ever get that feeling that you are lost with a hazy ghost like fog surrounding your body that just keeps growing?

That for some reason your body can't move on past the line of experiencing reality.

That there is always some form of demon swilling around your body, refusing to leave. You can't push them out because you can't grab hold of them. You can't understand them because you can't see them.

They start flying around your body faster and faster, turning your head into mincemeat. If you stop and even dare to think, even for a moment, that they will eat you alive and throw you back into the deep and take over your life.

Stage two, Depression.

Do you start to feel that your mind is corrupt and someone inside has been messing with all the wiring?

Do you ever believe that although everyone else exists in the same time zone, your life is in a Parallel universe?

That the concept of reality escapes you and you are just a buddle on lifeless bones?

That you must be doing this to yourself, and the reality of it happening cannot be true.

That the ghost filled mist that surrounds has taken control, taking away the senses of your human ability to live.

Stage three, Depression.

Do you ever just turn off?

Exist as a pile of bones and a shallow breather, nowhere?

Your name exists in time and space but the body and soul of the name has vanished

Do you ever have so little hope, life, will, that you don't move for days, weeks, and months?

Stage four, Depression

Nothingness – Depression

I do and this is my personal experience with Depression.

My rollercoaster had hit again in October 2012 with my mood generally getting worse and worse. It was deja vu from pervious experiences. Unfortunately, it felt like the therapy did not work, and my moods where back. I experienced extreme depression and suicidal thoughts. Not nice.

Suicidal

Why am I feeling so suicidal today, I am not sure I want to know
Smothered in dark clouds yet again, depressed is taking its toll

No matter how much I write or try to explain to myself
I just can't shrug of this feeling that I want to be dead

I have been looking up suicide again, I know it's hard to admit
But I am spiraling downwards out of control, into a demon ridden pit

I think I have been going down for a while, nothing seems to make sense
I am not even sure what it is I am going through but the fight is getting
intense

Everything is just so pointless, that I can't even think
My minds conjuring up these feelings but my heart just won't commit

I should not 20 question everything I feel, the pain is buried deep
I am struggling with wanting to live again as the depression takes a hit

I think that it is me, I have gone. I have disappeared in to space
All that I was has now passed on and depression has taken its place

Why stay being this person, a person that I don't even like.
Depression has taken hold of me and now it has taken my life

I generally don't want to live right now, I want these feelings away.
I have to go on for other people and hope depression won't stay

I do not like these feelings, I do not like this me
I know it is all seems so stupid, but please can you see

I want to die, I want to disappear
I hate that it is so difficult for other people to hear

THE SWING

So my moods began to swing from side to side creating a weather rollercoaster that no one would like to ride. Not only was I experiencing dramatic lows; these were then greeted again with dramatic highs. I would be springing around like a newborn lamb thinking up new plans and new ideas.

Fortunately, I was signed up on the Open University Psychology course, my eighth-degree and was rather committed to it. When I was low, I was unable to do or complete any course work, but when I was high I was a free flowing angel. I would work for hours and hours typing away, thinking that my work was a masterpiece. I would draw for hours thinking they would sell for millions, or I would write publishable poetry. I loved to be creative and on little sleep I would be up early in the morning painting trees or baking. I had a real obsession with trees and the way they grow into new life.

Night time was a little bit of a nightmare, though I didn't think so at the time and loved it all. Who needs to sleep when there is so much to do? I used to go out on midnight drives to a local hill. There, I would drive extremely fast around and around the outside. Luckily it was often 2am so no one was around, but it was not safe. I would then park up my little red car and look at the stars.

I have never wanted the Internet on my phone and know one could understand why. But as I sat there, looking up at the stars and having the Internet at a touch of a button, being able to buy anything I wanted, I was quickly in danger. I found out you could buy stars. Literally own a star in sky. Covertly, I now own about 50. This is why I never wanted Internet on my phone. I buy things, I buy stars whilst everyone else is tucked up in bed asleep.

Stars were not all I bought. I had massive spending sprees when I was on a high, something that Kate and I used to laugh about when I had come down. I bought and owned so many phones in such a short length of time I lost count. I owned 3 fully paid gym memberships in one year, which I bought in the space of one month. Never used any of the gyms. I also bought a brand new bike, again never used that either, but at least it's still around just in case.

The Internet quickly became a dangerous place as I spent hundreds of pounds quickly over a few weeks and never cared. Money seems to have no value, when you are high. It is just a means to an end. You want it; all you have to do is trade something in to get it, so you do it. Non-stop ideas run around your head thinking of all the brilliant things you can now do with any simple objects. These ideas over ride any thoughts around the money factor, and place money as invaluable. In fact there are no money thoughts just objects and a lust for that particular object. Albeit the night sky and the need to get fit was my lust when I was high.

Another issue of mine was I got a motor mouth that never shut up. The ideas in my head never stopped. I couldn't sleep and I used to get irritated at everything. People were so slow that I used to disconnect from them unless I needed something, which is completely uncharacteristic of me. I wouldn't text, but everyone knew I was either with the clouds or with the sun so understood.

I gained a tattoo on one occasion over Christmas. It is a bird on my left wrist, I cannot remember getting it, but the Christmas on 2012 I was very high. I was trying to hide it, very unsuccessfully though. I spent hundreds on Christmas presents and had such a brilliant time. I heard lots of voices of that Christmas saying that I was special and a celebrity. I used to walk into shop expecting everyone to know me or to kneel at my feet. I thought I was a leader of a brilliant story and the main character was I. Much like being a very happy and very popular Truman from the Truman show.

That as I remember was my last proper high. I did used to enjoy going high and having so much self-belief, but the pain when you get burnt by the sun is too much. Also the aftermath is such a mess and you have to spend your time cleaning it all up hoping another weather change is not going to happen quickly. All I prayed for was a stable mood. This is what I explained to my psychiatrist in January 2013

NEW DIAGNOSIS AND MEDICATION

In January 2013, shortly after Christmas and my last major high, I met with my new psychiatrist for the second time. Previously, I had had a quick appointment with one of his students and was asked to fill in a mood chart, like I have done many times before.

My new psychiatrist said he recognised me from my time in Underwood and me being under EIT. I cannot remember him from this time, which to me shows how unwell I was at that point in my life. If fact looking back I cannot remember anyone who saw me apart from my old care-coordinator.

The appointment went well, he looked at my charts and asked me some questions on my moods. I had Kate in there with me and she helped explain what he was asking me. I found it difficult to interpret what he was actually asking me so in turn how to give the most appropriate answer. I explained that my moods had settled down since being on Carbamazepine but felt it was wearing off and my moods were getting worse again. He took this on board and after examining my mood charts and listening to me gave me a diagnosis of Rapid Cycle Bipolar Disorder.

To this, I cannot lie; I was pleased with this diagnosis. Something I finally understood, something that explained my mood swings. I knew research on Bipolar and the definition behind it, so knew it was something treatable and manageable. This made me happy and thought I was finally able to start moving on with my life as soon as the words came out.

He decided to start me on Lithium and decrease all other medication apart from the Risperidone. I knew I was in for a bumpy ride, but did not care. Lithium was to be the answer: would this be the case?

Rapid cycles, Mixed Weather, Normality and grieving for an old weather change are four terms I am now more familiar with on a whole different level. Explanation - read on.

RAPID CYCLE

Although I found the new diagnosis a fit to my life, a few issues arrived which often took me a while to get my head around. One such case was the question which I found people were asking me since they knew my diagnosis. Friends and family already recognised that my moods cycled quickly without the diagnosis. They knew I could be cloud covered for a fortnight to be springing around in the next. It was only since my diagnosis that the question started to appear. I think this is because people knew the meaning of Bipolar so felt they could understand the answers I gave.

<u>"If your Rapid Cycling Bipolar, at least that means you won't
be in one state for too long, that's got to be a bonus right?"</u>

This is a statement had been running though my mind for a long time and I never quite knew where I stood on it. Positively, there lies some optimistic truth in the sentence, but mentally I am not sure. In any situation no one would like to feel depressed for a long period of time and seeing a light at the end of the tunnel can be a relief. But is it really that simple? I believe that cycling rapidly has a lot deeper roots than just looking for temporary relief.

At the moment I have 'rapid' cycled from very bright sunshine to the dark clouds but are now, fortunately, on the way up again. For the past few days I have lived through dark paralysing clouds and rainy thunderstorms battling each day to stay safe. I have hidden away in my bedroom becoming withdrawn from 'normal' life and just existing as a breathless pile on my bed. There has been no voice inside me or any will to exist but luckily this has only been for five days. It began slow on the Friday and gradually became worse until today, five days on; I can finally feel some sun through the cloud. My body is becoming less dragged down and I can gradually feel my heart beat again. As for a few days it has been awful, unbearable even. I have 'wasted' nearly a week of my life and have battle wounds to prove it.

I suppose I should look on the positive side: it is over, it was short lived. From my many times trapped in the clouds I can only begin to image how hard it must be for people to live that way for weeks, months or even years on end. But my time hasn't ended. It has just been broken. As for now, I am back on the lookout, hesitant to carry on living knowing I have to approach the next bend in my road and live through the next weather forecast. Although tiptoeing around my life is hard, looking back at past and remembering can be even worse. There is no way to change the past, likewise, no way to predict the future.

In contrast, I also cycle from the bright shining sun -from joy, laughter and warmth into the mellow party of life. Within five days I was able to book and rush off on a mini break to York; where I had a brilliant time laughing, walking and spending far too much. Back home I was lively, productive and magically creative until irritability, poor judgement and 'super human skills' set in. I had a brilliant time flying up into the sun until I began to get burnt. It took nearly two weeks until the sunset and the red sky at night set in. However, to remember all this, the way I felt in my mood, is where the pain really begins. If I was to look back two weeks today, my life feels so alien. How can you imagine yourself so full of life, so happy, without a care in the world to becoming just another normal human being? I had danced with the sun and seen the brighter side of life, but this had now gone. My moods became such a transformation in such a short space of time. But do I like it?

I feel I have come to the conclusion, that Rapid Cycle Bipolar isn't a bonus; it's a life you have to keep forgetting. You can't remember the highs when you're covered in deep dark clouds and you can't remember the lows when you're flying high with the sun. In addition, you cannot remember the weather or predict your future when the horizon is clear as the forecast is so uncertain. To be honest, I am not even sure that it's your own personal choice, to forget, it's more a process of the mind, of your sanity, a coping strategy to carry on.

<u>Another major problem of the Rapid Cycle Bipolar is if you remember the best bits, why would you bother doing anything on your low days?</u>

When you book things in, like a coffee with friends, it is hard to go when the clouds set in. Not only has your body begun to be dragged down, your inner voice whispers- 'why bother, in a 'few' days you could be normal, in fact maybe better than normal!' A dilemma is made, you could just wait and weather it out or put your life on hold again. If you do choose to continue you know that you will not be giving your best and it annoyingly it could make things worse. In the end, it is a personal decision and you have to pluck up the courage to continue with life. You have to force yourself to forget the 'clouds', the 'sun' and the 'normal' just to keep going. Even when it's hard, you have to stop searching for the light at the end of the tunnel and go with the flow. Rapid Cycling is definitely not a bonus, its section of an illness that needs coping with in its own right. Decisions on life need not to be based around the weather, more how to be a natural survivor. In conclusion, you have to keep going, whatever the weather.

MIXED WEATHER

<u>Mixed weather, mixed feeling and a mixed understanding of what is inside.</u>

Another issue that needs addressing with this diagnosis. I think these moods are known as mixed bipolar states but believe me they are not nice.

I was unsure what to write at the time or how to explain anything because I was unsure what I was feeling. I have left the following post unedited to how it was written at the time as it shows exactly what I was going though in March 2013.

I have recently began on my Lithium and was under the impression that all this craziness had passed; that I was on the road to recovery, a straight one. But now I see that my road is windy with dark tunnels and dead ends, not the yellow brick road that I was hoping for. I am sat here writing this at 3am and still feeling wide-awake; in company with a very annoying fly buzzing around me! I know that sleep is important, especially for me and is something I HAVE to keep intact, but still I have a little voice saying 'what is the point'.

"There so much to do: so many things that need doing. We are a mighty thought train tonight with new ideas being thrown on like luggage. Why stop that. Why sleep. There's no time"

I am by no means high as a kite right now but instead just soaring with the birds. I will get some sleep, eventually. I will close my eyes and let my imagination run wild with stories of magical lands. But right now I want to get some words on paper. I have been meaning to write for a while but words had disappeared from my mind as I swap and changing between a smile and a tear.

Recently, I feel like I have been trapped between two worlds. Between the sun and the clouds, I have been bouncing around, confusing my head to the max. I cycled in and out of depressive states for about three weeks. I thought I was on the yellow brick road of recovery but the weather keeps turning nasty. I would like to blame the reduction in medication, but it might have been inevitable. It has not been a nice few weeks, with voices shouting at me and the clouds coming in thick and fast but only staying for shorter periods. I manage to crawl out of their way, but am often left harmed by their impact.

The last week I have been neither here nor there. My mind and body have been skipping with the sun going on walks and seeing friends. But my soul feels like it's been burnt in the storm. I have broken down in tears on numerous occasions and I have ended up in A&E with the clouds covering my world. It's like the weather is always lingering inside me and I cannot seem to shake it off. Bolts of lightning hit me, piercing my head and destroying my thoughts. I fantasise about death and the wish upon the thoughts of the non-excitant 'life' I should of had. I curl up into a little ball waiting for the thunder of thoughts to stop. I scream in my head as they cripple me but the presence inside my body is strong. A few hours can pass and the sun will come through again, relieving my pain. I am able to go back down stairs and stay with other people like nothing has happened. I know they know that something was wrong, but nothing is spoken and we carry on like normal, until the lightning strikes again.

I feel like I have become haunted by my experiences. I feel like the weather has stuck to my insides and needs scraping out. I can still feel the pain of the bolts of lightning even though they have gone. I can feel myself crying and curling up in a ball even though I am not. I can feel the crippling pain that I was in. But I have no sensation, just a hunted memory that places me back in that pain. I feel like I never fully recovered from weather events, it's like they are too hard to process, too complicated to digest. I know that this always happens but this time particularly the mixed weather has stuck me down. Maybe it's because I have had an unusually stable mood beforehand and then it continues after with the experience being such short lived. It is as if spending time with the sun and then being thrown back into the clouds for a short period of time is not information my brain wants to process.

Thankfully I think the lightening ship is moving on and leaving me with blue skies and sunlight without their rude interruptions. However, my mind needed to get the mixed weather down on paper as it swishes round inside my head with no words and no meaning. I know this has happened before and its not clear-cut weather but it need to be recognised and sorted because it's pretty nasty stuff.

NORMALITY

Normality in all its glory is a very mixed up and muddled word. For me it's having the weather at either side and just having a clear blue sky ahead that creates my normality. When I can plan things, and think clearly I think I'm on to a winner. Living the dream for those weeks in time can be blessed. However walking down the weather indentation makes it very hard to interpret what's going on in my world. Rain to your left, sun shine to right means you've got to keep walking forwards and hope that neither of them will strike and tackle you down. But do you ignore them until they fully hit or do you take on their subtle hints of rapprochement and take repercussions? Do you label yourself each time you feel movement?

Being on a rapid weather cycle and getting better I feel I am consistently alerted to any silent tigers in my mood. If I start to get happy, talkative and activate then I slap on the sun cream getting ready for any possibility of mania. If I feel start to become low, feel tearful and want to be alone, then I put up my umbrella and question whether the depression clouds are coming in. The lines of distinction are thin and hard to tell when a side starts cracking. At the moment I'm not very good at quick reactions and wait for a cave in yet I feel I am at red alert all time. It is not just me but friends and family do too and I feel watched for any slight alterations in my mood. It seems that my bipolar has affected every thought and feeling that occurs, and every reaction inside and outside my body.

In a normal world, normal people have moods with highs and lows without severe weather reactions that can destroy their lives. People can live life without sun cream or umbrellas. People can live without the need to be constantly being aware of their thoughts and feelings all the time. Since starting on Lithium my moods have begun to stable out. I have had less time flying in the sky with the sun and less time in the deep dark clouds. Now the time has come for me to experience normality but with this normality comes a life in limbo. I am never quite sure weather I am on a cycle of blue-sky mood before the weather comes in or how long it will last. Labels seem to be finding their place in my life, with a crack on the side comes in a possibility of hypomania or depression. I'm finding that I am learning to live with the subtle weather changes and it is just as traumatic as having learnt to overcome with full-blown storms. Although I'm living a life in limbo I need to remember that I am not a machine and not every crack means distracter.

At the moment, I am always feeling guilty of being in a normal mood because I am constantly looking over my shoulder for the next change. This acceptance of normality is strange for me and I don't know what to do, or how to feel. The built in fear that the weather has left behind, tackles my normal self but I don't want the ridge hold of the ghosts to stay forever. This is an issue I never thought of and I don't think many do. Bipolar is associated and defined as mood difficulties. And yes that's true and it's a symptom of the illness that makes up that definition. But it is much more as its takes hold of your body. Mania and depression are the main symptoms, but normal blue-sky mood should be in there to. As when you're walking down that blue sky path you will forever have a sword and shield in either hand ready to fight off the approaching weather. Normality will never just be normal; there will always be sun cream and umbrellas handy. I believe it's how you live with those weapons and accessories that will determine your normality. I just have to learn how to use them to keep me on the track of walking forward into the blue sky.

MISSING MY WEATHER ROLLERCOASTER

As life goes on I am starting to miss my weather symptoms as other, older symptoms take their place into the mix. On a somewhat positive note I had some great results on Lithium. For once my mood seems to be stabling out and I didn't have as many extreme highs or lows for a while. Unfortunately, I was coming to realise that I was really missing the hyper manic states I had experienced. I loved being able to get everything done, feeling brilliant, rushing with creativity and have huge self-confidence. Now I am plain sky and being of normal mood a lot of the time I cannot get that buzz and nothing quite tops it.

My mood at the moment is more like a child's rollercoaster, still more extreme then most but manageable. Regrettably however, my perception of myself has changed and I think a key part of this is missing out on the unexpectedness of the weather changes but most importantly the highs. Even the extreme highs where I thought I was famous, hearing voices, commands and bursting with self-belief give me a tingling to my brain I miss. This seemed to happen in Lancaster too. That when the Carbamazepine started to work my psychological self came down hill.

Obviously, it is better that these episodes are discontinued however, my new smaller rollercoaster has brought with it its own psychological issues. I think a huge impact is that the high part of me seems to exist no more and I no longer have those feelings of being alive. The feelings of tingling and self-important moments have gone and I'm left bland and self-critical. I miss it personally but on a deeper level I think my brain misses it to. Links like this make me accept the diagnosis even more as little things seem to fit into place.

Unfortunately, I seemed to have developed a very anxious and self-punishing personality in response to losing my identity - my moods. The metaphor I used to explain what was going on for many years and the implications became my identity. But now as I would like to move away from that, my evil head won't let me. I want to live with my condition not live as my condition. My brain won't leave me alone shouting insults and putting me down all the time. I always believe it and it's creating a wide-open trap which I'm falling into it head first. I seem to have lost my confidence and I think it's because I have lost my identity. I no longer have high times which enabled me to pick myself up and love myself for a bit. Kate and others informed me of this crisis that I would encounter as my Bipolar came under control. It is included in bipolar texts and websites but no-one seemed to explain the feeling behind it.

The acceptances of normal moods swings into your life are a dilemma of their own right. Normal life has become foreign to me and I don't think I'm coping well. I think I am grieving for my highs and now I have more time to be around myself and in my own company without the weather changes, the more I'm struggling. It's all playing games with my head and im starting to find simple things hard, as the torture from my mind gets worse. I seem to be beating myself up all the time, the nasty voices I hear have got worse and I have had many breakdowns. Not necessarily all caused by my moods but by not understanding my life anymore. I suppose I expected to stable out and be able to move straight on with my life and gain a new identity. Maybe even the identity I lost. But it is not like that; in fact it's a million miles away.

On the whole without my hyper manic state my confidence has gone, and without my weather so has my identity. I am in a mixed up world now and need to find a space to fit myself in again. I fought so hard to get rid of the illness, which took so much away from me as a student, that I think I have lost who I am. In a strange way I miss my weather, which is horrible thing to admit, but it was a familiar turmoil that I was used to. Now having silently more predictable moods has brought a basket full of problems, some that I have experienced before and they have come up and bitten me again.

THE WEATHER MOVES ON

As the weather becomes to be controllable though Lithium therapy, it has given my brain a new chance to process everything else which isn't quite normal. Yes, I have a diagnosis of Bipolar and Multiple Personality Disorder, but this is not the end of my symptoms. Unfortunately, over the next few months old symptoms seem to start appearing again and taking control. It is easy to see that once my moods become under control that I have another psychological cause underlying everything.

> *It is important to recognise that at this stage in life I do not accept my diagnosis of multiple personality disorder. This is why, there is nothing written on this diagnosis – yet!*

I started Lithium in January 2013 in hope that it would be a cure to the weather rollercoaster I was experiencing. To begin Lithium therapy you have to go through various tests to make sure you body can cope with the medication. These included: blood tests, urine test and an ECG. Lithium is a type of salt that you are putting in to your body, it needs to closely monitored to make sure that your blood level is at the therapeutic dose. This requires 3 monthly blood tests for life to keep an eye on kidney level function and to make sure that the medication is not poisoning you. Everything was good with my results from the preliminary tests, so I was able to start on Lithium quickly. Lithium again is based and monitored via the blood. It needs to be at a therapeutic level to work, which is another reason of the routine bloods. I liked this about the medication as it means it's dose do not need uncalled for increases if I was to have a mood swing, as they could see things from a science level.

NAMING OF THE DISSOCIATION EPISODES

Three months in to Lithium therapy, I was finally starting to see an improvement in my mood and it seemed that Lithium was my miracle cure. My rollercoaster was settling down and I could finally start functioning in life. I was still on Risperidone to keep my voices at bay so everything seemed to be running well.

In late March 2013, I decided I was well enough to go to York to visit my friend, my only friend from university, Darcy. We met up at the train station and stayed one night in a very nice B&B. It was lovely seeing her and we literally did not stop talking and laughing all day and all night. I had a brilliant time. I suppose I was a little hyper manic looking back, but that was fine and I had fun and a newfound freedom. I caught all the train there and back all by myself that lasted for 2 hours each journey, so I was proud to become independent again. It wasn't until I got home that my world turned upside down, never to be returned.

Unfortunately, I acquired an ear infection in York that was sore and painful. On the week of my return I found it hard to go out of the house because of the wind and my ears. It did not bother me too much, and didn't cause the demons to pay a visit. I arranged to see my friends from the psychology group therapy at a local café called The Barn for a coffee. Finally getting out of the house, I drove the 20 minutes journey singing away to Meatloaf without a care in the world. Little did I know that would be the last time I drove anywhere for the unforeseeable future.

As soon as I got to the Barn, I did not feel right. My head was fuzzy and I felt rather light-headed. It was as though I was having warning signs of a dissociative episode that I had been experiencing a lot recently. I sat down, and wasn't worried. My friends had seen me have these episodes before so I knew they would not panic and knew what to do. The problem is I was not coming out of it. I had gone pale and sweating and couldn't respond to anyone. I really was not well. My eyes kept going blurry and I was unable to talk to say what was going on. I felt awful and so disconnected from the outside world. It was lasting for over an hour so my friends decided to phone my parents to come pick me up.

My dad came and collected me from The Barn but I still was not coming round. With the help of my friends we left my car on a road outside the barn and my dad drove me home where my mum was waiting. At the time they were not worried has I had had many of these episodes throughout my life, but when my mum saw me and realised I was not coming round they decided something was not right. Both my patents took me to A&E that night. I was seen in the non-critical care unit, not A&E and they assumed I had a virus due to my ear infection. I had blood taken and was given a prescription for antibiotics and then sent on my way.

Strangely enough, on the way home I came round. I bounced back to being normal again: this was no virus. I kept being well for an hour or two before going into another trancelike state. This was to be my life for the next week.

I spent the next few days curled up on the sofa. Not watching TV or having any music on, just being there. I was not depressed, I was not suicidal, I am not even sure what I was, I just was not there. All I remember is getting blurry vision then losing gaps of time. I see pictures a lot when I am normal, but these were taking a completely different form. I had scenes of strange things on a cycle going through my mind. For example: people climbing out of graves, mice on cheese blocks or bouncing balls in an empty room. They would just keep flashing up one after the other causing me to disconnect from the world. I was just in my own sense of reality, unable to do or focus on anything.

Three days on and things were getting no better, so we visited a doctor at our local walk-in centre. Whilst I was there I had one of my attacks where I would just stare vacantly into space and be cut off. People can wave arms in front of me, hit me or do anything and I would not responsed. The Doctor saw one of these episodes and suggested I went straight to A&E. So my mum took me there and a doctor saw us straight away.

The doctor who came was so nice and caring. He conducted neurology tests and found everything to be ok, he then began to asked me some questions and I had another attack. I stared blankly into space and did not move. I don't know what happened in the period of time but when I came round he explained to me that he believed I was having absent seizures. He phoned a neurologist in another local hospital and they recommend that I was to be admitted and for various tests to be done.

HOSPITAL

In the end I spent three nights in hospital that were anything but fun. I was admitted on the Friday so things where slow to happen over the weekend. I was not sent for any tests but the Doctors kept saying I was going to be sent for a CT scan. The query diagnosis kept changing from brain tumour to epilepsy to unknown so everything was so confusing. I can remember looking at walls, seeing them change colours and move.

Whilst I was there I found it very difficult to sleep. I was moved to a medical ward that was also the stroke ward for observation. On my second night there was confusion over me taking my Lithium and it wasn't until 3 am that I was allowed to take it. This however, I believed helped me recover.

As I said I found sleeping hard. I had all these moving pictures and kept going into trancelike states that I couldn't turn off, in turn making me only able to lucid dream. Lucid dreaming is horrible, I don't know why people try and train themselves to achieve it. It is especially horrible in hospital when there are so many things going on. I was in a lucid dream state at 3 am after I had finally got to 'sleep'. A nurse came over for me to take my medication, as the Lithium had finally been hospital prescribed. She nudged me, in hopeful of a quiet and gentle awakening, instead I screamed. She really scared me that much that I sat bolt up right and screamed in her face, it was horrid and she made me jump so high. She was so apologetic though and so nice as she gave me Lithium and helped calm me down. When I finally had my soul back in my body I closed my eyes. Amazingly all the pictures had stopped, everything had disappeared. It was as if she had literally scared it out of me. I managed to fall back asleep, I would not say peacefully, but at least I was no longer lucid dreaming.

The next day, it would have been nice if I had woke up refreshed but I didn't. I was still having seizures, but the pictures had disappeared. I fainted twice that day, but what was strange is on the second faint I lost my voice. I could not talk at all. Cough; sneeze, hum, nothing came out. An hour later, eventually it did sound came back, but it was not my voice. It was high and squeaky, something I had never experienced before. Because of this a neurologist came to see me, and the diagnosis of epilepsy was then hanging over my head. I was told I could not drive for the foreseeable future and that I would be sent to see my old neurologist again for tests on an outpatient's basis. With this, I was discharged, scared and felt I was still unsure what was actually going on. Things were not better and I felt I didn't have an answer.

For the next few weeks, my voices took turns and tumbles as it went from being none existent. To jibber jabber, to a high voice or a whisper. I kept having disconnected episodes and attack, plus fainting on regular basis. I waited months for an appointment to come through with no avail. Eventually, we decided to go private.

A Sleep and dreaming a poem

It 2 am and I am wide awake
Everyone else is tucked up in bed
It's not that I can't sleep; it's more about my dreams
where are these visions of sugar plums that I used to believe

I used to sleep like a baby, have dreams so sweet
But now they torture my mind and take defeat
I cannot rest as I lucid dream
Taking control of my mind, sleep isn't what it seems

True I have been out for a couple of hours
But these have been twisted, horrible, everything sour
It's like I cannot turn off, nor can I rest
Dreams become something I sadly regret

My dreams are on repeat, my minds on replay
I hallucinate pretty badly before going into this way
Colours start flashing, pictures appear
As soon as I close my eyes, my nightmare begins

Twisting my body until I break
My dreams are so nasty they force me awake.
Sadly I have to get up for some rest
When all that I want is to be tucked up in bed

It's hard to open my eyes but unfortunately I know
That the other way is to be trapped in their horror show
So I take a break and do some colouring in
Have a drink of herbal tea knowing I have to believe

That when I go back to bed in the next few hours
Lucid dreaming will have stopped, my sleep won't be sour
I have to stay strong, return to my bed
Rest my tired little eyes and this sleepy head

I pray that when I wake the sun will be shining
That morning has returned and my final hours were brighter
However if I awake and my clock reads 4 am
Then the nightmare has repeated and show has started again.

THE INVESTIGATION

As the weeks went on; my symptoms became more and more varied, strange and extreme. I went from walking sideways, being unable to walk, to being sick after everything I ate. My symptoms would come on for weeks at a time, then change or disappear. This had happened all my life, for symptoms to be strange and go on for weeks to only to disappear when I finally got persuade to visit the doctors. In addition my disconnected episodes were still happening and to the extreme.

They start with my eyes going blurry. This can happen when I am talking to someone, watching TV, reading or just in any situation really. I then become disconnected for around 10 to 15 minutes, where I stare blankly into space, not in reality and unable to communicate with anyone. No one can get my attention and it is as if I don't exist for that time. When I come back to reality, I cannot remember what has gone on. It then takes a while for me to return to normal. Around 10 to 20 minutes I can be partly here, partly not. I often can't talk, or if I can it does not make sense, all nonsense talk. When I return to functioning normal, I cannot remember the entirety of what has happened but my head feels amazing and I feel like I can now think clearly again.

Sounds like a seizure, well that's what everyone thought. Having waited 3 months we finally decided to go private and visit the Neurologist who had diagnosised me with Hemiplegic Migraines in 2012. I saw him on a Saturday morning and it cost me £300 which was well worth it. Again he did the neurological tests on me and then sent me for an MRI and an EEG that were performed on the NHS. I was then sent back to see him on the NHS waiting list.

I know this sounds slightly unfair, that I went for private treatment to be referred back into the NHS and was able to be seen faster. But I had been discharged from hospital and ditched. My GP was trying everything to get me seen quicker but the waiting list for initial assessment was so long, so paying was the best way forward. My symptoms were not nice and were stopping me having a normal life. I had had ambulances called out twice and been to A&E as a result. No one seemed to be giving me any answers.

So an MRI of my head was conducted, along with a sleep deprivation EEG. I was then back to see the Neurologist a month later to get my results. This was the one of hardest appointments of my life. I was assuming as I sat outside in the waiting room that he was going to tell me I had epilepsy. This I had come to terms with and felt quite settled with as a diagnosis. However what he said to me, on a personal note was much worse.

The neurologist explained that after viewing the results of the tests and watching videos of my seizures he decided they were functional in nature not epileptic. This I was supposed to be happy about and I think he expected a smile; instead he got tears. He continued to diagnose me with Conversion Disorder. A disorder I was familiar with because of Lucy's experience. A disorder which I dreaded that the outcome was going to be. A disorder that I did not want but sadly knew it made sense.

Snippet in my mind - Poem - This is I

Yes I have a mental illness
But I won't let it define me
True I am mentally unstable
Yet that gives a nice variety

I find it hard to cope
With situations others find easy
But everyone has a breaking point
Mine just appears a little early

Please excuse me as I battle on
But my plans have had to change
I am just trying to find myself
And stop hiding from the pain

Milly Jones

I bear my symptoms hoping to find
A more likeable me and an acceptance inside
So here I go and dive within
This won't be pleasant, this may be grim

Voice in music and Music in silence
All spoken so real that their trickery becomes cane
The same with those bugs and those mystery people
And the flashing up picture and creepy moving video

Those ticks that make me squeak
And my inability to talk
Turning my emotional pain physical
Often causing me to stall

Invading my head, thoughts aren't always my own
Whispering evil plans they take control
Sometimes they chant, sometimes they sing
But what is real life, I'm not sure who to believe

So yes l self harm, Yes I am suicidal
Yes I cry with my insides dying
Yes I fall apart on a regular basis
But consider all this my mental illness

My arms are so scarred with my battle wounds
I am a practicing ninja so please do excuse
But this will not stop me, I will not give in
Even if this means if I don't always win

Yet with all this going on
Life is never that simple
But if I Just take a peep
And I can still find that sparkle

I am determined to carry on
And I love to be happy
Laughing and giggling
Makes my whole life worthwhile

So Yes I am different
Yes I am unique
But my life is very triggering
Yet I live with all this

Realising my symptoms might never go
Then combining them with me, I take control
I have mental illness, but it does not define
My life is unique, I am not ready to hide

EXPLANATION OF CONVERSION DISORDER

Conversion Disorder in my case consisted of non-epileptic seizures and being thrown back in time. It is explained as emotional distress turned in to physical symptoms. It is a problem with the software in the body causing real and painful symptoms just as intense and life damaging as physical problems.

Everyone has experienced some aspect of conversion disorder. You know that feeling of sickness before an exam, those jellybeans jumping around in your tummy before a driving test. You may actually be sick with nerves when the emotional distress of an upcoming exam gets too intense. This is conversion, emotional distress causing physical symptoms. You cannot control it, nor can you help it, it is your body's way of letting out stress.

Many people have also experienced some kind of dissociative episode, which is like my non-epileptic seizures, and are linked with conversion disorder. Have you ever driven a well-driven route, for example to work, got there and realised you cannot remember the drive? Or have you ever been on autopilot and made a cuppa in the morning, sat down and not remembered making it? Both of these are small samples of dissociation.

Like any disorder, Conversion Disorder is diagnosis when the symptoms are out of control and disturbing your life. At the time and for the last few years I have found it hard to function because of dissociative episodes and conversation disorder. My main symptoms of the disorder at this time include: non-epileptic seizures, being sick, left sided weakness and voice problems. There are more, but it starts to get confusing

CONVERSION DISORDER, MY VIEW

I am sat here cocooned on my little bed with a blanket wrapped round me. My room is clean and tidy, nothing out a place, everything sat in the correct position. The room looks perfect as I look out on it, yet for the last few weeks it has been my hiding place. The room were I can release in silence, undisturbed. I sit here in my bedroom, not with the TV on, not with music on but instead in the quiet. I can hear voices; hear demons calling me into the darkness. I can feel my soul clinging on but ever so often it detaches itself. A seizure; Dissociation; Conversion Disorder. My mind unable to process anything, unable to keep covered all the buried thoughts and feelings instead go. Disappearing for some time until it has found a bigger boulder to keep things under. Locked away, out of sight, out of mind

To look at me, I may seem well; A pawn in the book of life. But inside I am frightened. Frightened to keep living and keep control of my life. Fighting to keep my head above the water and not slip into the world of disconnecting. It is now as I sit cocooned on my bed that I can fully reflect the damage my mental health brings to my physical health. My brain leaves me with a bruised body and a beaten up soul. The thoughts that I am unable to speak make my body move in ways that I don't understand. The emotions I feel cause my body to disconnect and leave me without a voice or any sound to be made. Inside it sometimes feels like my soul is jumping around like spring lambs trying to escape the pain. My brain disconnects creating a feeling of freeness and carelessness when it finally reconnects to my body. I feel better and can think clearer when my body has taken the brunt of my mental illness.

The impact on the world means my body eats away at any joyful living I have as I am scared of what will happen next. Everything is unpredictable from being sick for weeks on end, to having seizures and losing control of my voice. This is combined with playing with the sun or being lost in the clouds. I am not sure whether I am coming or going. I know I am lost, without a way to stop any of these things from happening. I use sensation, and hold a teddy, take some pills to stop the weather. Some things may look strange, but it stopped me from scratching my skin raw, just to regain some control as I reverted back to childhood coping strategies.

Unfortunately, I do not recognise myself anymore, since this all began. I do not know this creature on my bed and things my body can do. My mental health makes me afraid of my own head, but now in turn makes me afraid of my own body. I find it hard to see past the dark shadow that has encased my body and soul. A great pain and hurt has arisen from within and all I have to do is think about having no control. I feel like a shell that once was. I cannot see me anymore. Conversion Disorder has taken its toll; I cannot see how to take back the control it has taken away. But believe you me, I am trying and every time something happens, I learn from it and build up new ways to cope.

SNIPPET IN MY MIND - FEELING GUILTY

It's July 2013 and nothing seemed to make sense, everything I experienced had a psychological twist that could not be justified. I feel guilty for wanting a reason for my problems because somehow that would be easier. A scan to show what's gone wrong; an image to show some damage; a recording of the sounds of the people I hear. Without this proof I feel I am nothing. I find it hard to believe anything of my life because there are no facts behind it.

How can I feel the pain of the smothering clouds or the glowing sun when there is no trigger around to create it?

How can my moods be such a soul destroying problem, impacting me so much in my life that I can't even remember what it feels like when I'm not experiencing them?

Why do I lose my voice and speak incoherent language when my brain's supposedly working perfectly?

Why do I disconnect from time and space when there is nothing around to cause it?

Why can't I believe my own thoughts, my own feeling, my own body reaction to myself?

Why do I hear music when none is around?

Hear voices inside and outside my head that no one else can hear?

See people who are not there?

Have walls and floors change colour or move?

Why do I hallucinate at night and control my dreams all the time in a lucid dreaming state?

I want to know the truth but I am scared that there is no reason. What justification do I have with no proof that I am not causing my own mental illness.

DRIVING

After the Easter weekend of 2013, I lost my driving licence. Both the hospital and my psychiatrist said I was unsafe and unfit to drive; my freedom taken away. I had driven since I was 17. I know lots of people live without a car, which made me feel so guilty for feeling that my life was being taken away. Yet my car was a part of me, my life.

In the recent years driving had become my life: driving up to see my friends at the Barn or completing a ceramics course all made me feel free. I loved escaping for days out and going for cakes and drinks of tea with friends past and present. I was keen and always eager to be the one to drive whenever we went out as it gave me a sense of purpose. I have to admit when I was ill, manic, I was a danger. But this was under control now thanks to my Lithium therapy.

I was the first one to drive at 17, taking people on trips and giving them lifts everywhere. I mentioned I used to go to drive to supermarkets with my best mate, or go and get an ice cream on sunny days. I used to love going on late night drives just for the sake of it. Many of my friends still lived in my university towm, so driving was my connection to them, to their life, to my old life. Driving gave me a sense of independence at a young age and I was good at it. I am a confident driver and use the time as me time. Time to sing along to the radio, and become trapped in my own little bubble

It is the seizures that were the issue. The problem is I cannot recognise when I am going into one. I just disconnect from time and space when it happened, unable to function, that makes me very unsafe to drive. Even I can admit it but did not want to believe it. It felt like my freedom was taken over night and that it would be an impossible task of even getting out of the house. It felt like I would become trapped, unable to function.

I know this sounds like an over reaction, but my car was my life. Luckily it was found that this was not the case.

Like everything in my life, I got through the tunnel and out the other side. With help from my amazing GP, I applied and received a bus pass that allowed me free travel free on public transport. I also began walking everywhere and loved listening to my music being able to escape from everyone. Having no car as it turned out was not so bad. Getting around was a little harder and more time consuming, but I was not working and was hardly in a rush to go anywhere. Looking back it was more a blessing in disguise and I managed to lose 3 stone in a year and become more independent then I ever was in a car.

I started to accept my life and kept battling on; again, this was not going to destroy me.

SNIPPET - MY EXPERIENCE OF DISSOCIATION

I once had an augment in a philosophy lecture about time. If the universe only existed as a box then there would be no time; time would be infinite. This makes complete sense to me, but everyone else in class argued that I was wrong and misunderstood. 'How can time not exist, there has to be time if there is a universe.' I debated back that if the universe only existed as a box and nothing changed then what would time be measuring? There would be no need for time as nothing would change; hour by hour, minute by minute or second by second. Therefore, if the universe was a box there would be nothing to measure and time would be infinite. It does not matter if there is a universe; if nothing changes then there is no time.

I feel this applies to me sections of my life, inside me. Time for me can sometimes seem to exist as this box, I can hold the universe. I have a magical power that enables me to disconnect myself from time and space. I can escape for minutes or hours only to be brought back and return to time and life. My mind goes into a separate compartment; hiding away in my universe box. This for me is my experience of dissociation a part of conversion and multiple personality disorder.

Within my head there are many locked boxes and separate compartments in which I hide. It is like my head is designed for only me to live in although I am not sure of my way around. It is a complete web of a tortured mind and provides protection when there is no danger and harm when there is no need. It is like the flight and fight mechanism is on auto drive and kicked in at 100%. When I fly, I fly into a box: a universe box. When inside the box, it denies me of time, memory and real sensation.

Sometime the box flips and swallows me whole without warning, other times; I can feel it sucking my soul out, like the dementors on Harry Potter.

When inside the universe box, I do not exist in time anymore, no seconds, no minutes and no hours. My state of mind does not change so there is no time to measure. Outside I am blank, there is no me, no life, no human. To on lookers it looks like a seizure, a blank stare as my mind seems to be piecing things back together. To me it is nothingness. I have blurry eyes before I am trapped, then my voice and all my abilities to function as a human goes. I have no life, no actions to measure inside. I am often in this state for at least 15 minutes, where I am trapped by the box and time dose not exist. Afterwards I have a lull period for a varied amount of time. In this space I can often see things going on and try to interpret what is happening but my mind won't let me. Everything feels like a slow moving video and that my time is separate from yours. I am trying to cry out, to function but I can't understand what people are saying. Questions just have no meaning, even if it is simple. My brain cannot process information as I crawl out from my box trying to adjust to living time again and speed things up to a normal setting. Trapped in this box, I am experiencing dissociation as it swallows and bundles me in. I often have no memory recall of being in the box, so how could there be any time for me?

Recently these episodes have had another twist; Pain. The box has become sharp, jagged edged and glass in the bottom. It feels like I am being thrown back to previous memories and that someone, something is causing me pain. The pain makes my body tremble, re-living some kind of painful memory making my muscles tense up and agonising hurt all over my body. I know I reassure myself by coming away damaged as I scratch myself trying to turn my pain into something I understand. Instead of having a painful body for no reason, I self harm unconsciously so that I have some control. At this point of time, I am neither in nor out of my box. I am floating, swimming around my head and space trying to grasp onto something I understand. Time as other people know it does not exist within me at this time. I am thrown back into a memory, into a time I can't escape, a time that is not real anymore.

If the universe was a box, and time was discontinued then no one would be living. We may not die; we would just be paused in space and time with nothing changing second by second, minute by minute. This is my experience of dissociative episodes in my head but I know not the reality. I come round in places where I did not disappear, moved in my absence of time. The universe is not a box for others, and time continues for them whilst I am in my state of non-existence, disconnected. Perhaps that is why my class could not understand something which seemed so obvious to me. I could not comprehend how you could argue the point that if something exists there has to be time. I thought it was normal to lose time and become absent from the world, to be pulled into a box.

Descartes', a famous philosopher, once quoted 'I think, therefore I am'. When I dissociate and disconnect, I don't think, therefore I am not. If I am not, and nothing changes then there is no time. I become the box, the universe, nothing exists, nothing will ever exist or be remembered of that time, therefore that time did not exist.

Complicated?

SNIPPET IN MY MIND - A LETTER TO MYSELF

Dear Milly,

There are many questions I would like to ask you but just don't hear. There never seem to be the right time to sit you down and bombard you with the thoughts that fly around my head. I don't understand your working, your tick-tocking processing life or your view of the world. Why do you change your mind so rapidly from a world of sun and roses to a life of suffering?

We are supposed to get on together, to live in harmony but you seem to have your own separate life, your own control. I try my best to push on though and to make a world that's right for me but somehow you always seem to destroy it. How is it that I don't know what you think or what you feel. How is it that you fill me up with such strange sensations and that I feel there is no way out. Why do you fail me? Why do you argue with me? Why can I never just have my own thoughts, my own life without you interfering and bullying me?

We could love life and have so much joy, but you turn around and pull us back down. I thought we were getting it right, I thought we were beginning to get along but then you go and destroy it again. You have now started to fail me physically and as if by magic the witty comments and bullying sounds return. I feel I have already lost my mind, but please not my body too. Why do you hate me? Why can't we just get along?

Be normal.

We would be great together. We could achieve stuff and have a brilliant life I just know it. But with you playing your stupid games of seizures and madness I don't know where we are heading for. I am lost and the outlook looks dim. I don't know what to believe with you anymore. I don't know what I want to believe of you anymore. It's like I say one thing and you do the other. This is not a relationship and it's clearly not working. I hate what you think, but I'm starting to hate you. How do we move on with this, will you shut up and stop playing your games?

I think if we work together we could achieve peace. I'm tired now, of fighting, of thinking I'm winning to being slammed back down. I'm tired of feeling I have lost my mind, lost my body. So please can we learn to get on. Let's start talking to each other and gain some consistency in our life.
Let's work together – A final plead.

Yours truly,
Yourself!

AMERICA

I am a keen traveller; before I got ill I managed to go around India with two of my close friends. This may have been where my problems started to arise again since sixth from, but it does not stop the love of travelling that is inside my body. In 2013, I was lucky enough to go to America and Canada for 3 weeks, but this was not without it's problems.

Earlier in the year before my seizures started I had decided to go inter-railing with my best friend Jenny. We had picked a route which went through Budapest, Bratislava, Vienna and Prague. I had help organise getting the train tickets and we were in our finally stages managing to book the hotels. Unfortunately, mental health is not predictable, even if your feeling well one month to book a travelling holiday I have now learnt that does not mean you will be able to go on it. Regrettably, my seizures were getting worse, although my moods were under more control they were still ruling my life. Stress I know is a big factor so that more I thought about the holiday and what could go wrong with me whilst I was out there, the more I worried.

Adventurously, I made one of my hardest decisions and had to call off the holiday. My main worry was Jenny would not enjoy herself being with me whilst I was still having so many seizures and my mood being still at an unpredictable level. This was in June and we were due to go in the August. Unfortunately, we did lose some money from our hotel booking and I thought at the time that maybe I may have lost a friend. However, Jenny is amazing and nothing was mentioned of it again once all the cancellations had come through.

I still needed a break though and in June shortly after cancelling our holiday I book another one with my parents. Some maybe confused with this but I know that my parents can cope with me. They live with me; know the sliding down the door crying moments, know what to do if I have seizure and most of all, I know they will never leave me. I was apprehensive about booking such a long trip worried that I may stress my parents out but the plan was good.

We decided to fly to LA and hire a car to make the 2500 miles drive to Vancouver stopping off places on the way (well, kind of on the way). The holiday was amazing and I had a brilliant time. I found it a lot easier to cope with than other holidays because we were in the car most of the day. We would get up earlier and travel in the morning stopping for lunch at some fantastic places such as Monterey and Big surf. We saw wild whales, sea lions and otters from our car window and took in the American culture as we visited some unique towns on the way. I was lucky enough to step inside, and drive through a tree when we saw the red woods, see rare wild birds when visiting "Crater lake". The weather was not too hot but enjoyable and every evening we would have to drive around trying to find somewhere to stay. For 6 days we had no booked accommodation so replied on hostel at the road side or tried to book places for the next night using the internet.

We drove through Portland to Seattle where we left the car. As I previously said I had been to Seattle before, and the memories came flooding back. I have a strange wiring for memories and often get thrown back in to the situation I remember as if I was there again. Sometime this is good, sometimes this is bad. For Seattle it was ok, although things kept creeping up on me that I had to block out - which I did quite successfully. After two nights in Seattle we caught the train to Vancouver where we were met straight away by my brother.

My eldest brother, David, is 8 years older than me and I can't remember much about growing up with him. I hadn't seen him for at least three years and in this time he had made a family. This was the first meeting of his little girl, Ariel and his little boy, Ben. Ariel was 3 on this first meeting with her and so full of life. I immediately warmed to her and she definitely wasn't a shy girl. Ben was only 18 months and a lot quieter but had the cutest little smile. I hadn't really been around children before meeting these two so was a little nervous, but that quickly went. I can't believe how easy it was to play with Ariel, she told you what to do and if you were doing it wrong. I enjoyed every moment with her and it made me sad that they all lived so far away.

It was great to see David too. I felt we had a lot to catch up on but it was hard with the children there to entertain all the time. Luckily on the last day we got some time together whilst he was on a dinner break from work. He seemed to be enjoy living in Canada and was making a success of himself. He was coping well with his family and enjoyed being a dad so that made us all happy. We only spent four days in Vancouver with them before flying home.

Overall the trip was a huge success and I thoroughly enjoyed my time. My seizures were still happening but a lot less frequently. My mood seem to be stabling out even if I did have a few crying moment. On the plane on the way back I still agreed with myself that cancelling the Europe trip was the right decision. I agree with that to this day. It's hard to explain, but when you know you can't do something, you just know.

CHANGE OF MEDICATION

Unfortunately, when I got home, things changed again. Initially, I was doing at a lot better and I thought that things were finally starting to pick up for me. I had arranged some volunteer work at a local hospital that I was looking forward to getting started. I also began to attend a local café that helped people with mental health difficulties and thought all my symptoms were finally becoming under control.

I attended a psychiatrist appointment on 7th October 2013 and to be honest nothing has ever been the same since. I explained that things were going well and I had been to America and things seemed to be heading in the right direction. At the time I was on Lithium and Risperidone. I had been on Risperidone for quite a while by then, over 5 years, but it was working well. I really like it as a drug because I knew that if my voices got bad I could take an extra dose and it would really help. I also knew it helped me sleep. Regrettably, Risperidone was having a negative effect on my Prolactin levels in my blood. My psychiatrist decided that because of the diagnosis of bipolar he would change this anti psychotic to Quetiapine, a more recognised drug used to treat bipolar. He explained that it would help me sleep and also keep my mood lifted.

I trusted him. So I agreed to change.

Unfortunately, Quetiapine does not work for me, as I was about to find out!

CRISIS TEAM WEEK OCTOBER 2013

Today l feel like I am going to explode. Here is a little snippet into my world. I have come off Risperidone after the psychiatrist decided to swap it for Quetiapine due to recent blood results. It has been days since I was on the lower dose and the crisis team have become involved. My mind is running at the speed of light, l keep hearing scratching noises and my head's buzzing and feels funny. I feel like I want to do everything but I have no energy to move. My mind is racing but all I want to do is sleep. That I am balancing on the sane and insane tightrope, going into the depth of the mixed mood feeling again.

I feel sad, I feel happy, I feel despair. I want to live but l also wanted to die. Feeling a Bipolar mixed state does not even come close to explain how much my mind is running with psychotic symptoms. But what is even more annoying is l feel so irritated. Annoyed at everything, little things, people are frustrating me. What is more infuriating is that I am annoyed at being annoyed. I want to talk to people, to mix with society but my head doesn't want to shut up. The inside and the outside voices wont be quiet for even one second. They abuse me and say things I don't want to hear. l can recognize that that is me getting annoyed with me and other people actually annoying me. But its so annoying. I want to be free flowing. Have an endless train of thoughts coming from my mind. Hovering is what im doing. Trying to remain normal, settled, not out of place. Stable. Sane. Run. Sleep. Usually l would take a Risperidone but they're all gone. Bye Bye down the hole, should of taken more. Should be writing a personal statement. It would be wonderful, enlightening but l can't do it. Blockage. Writers block. How can l write a sane piece of work? Not with this head, not with these people. I feel I can see the future but I can't see me in it. I want to run away from it. Hide. My mind wants to exist in time and space but my voices, my body doesn't. It is an endless battle of wills with weapons being used. To live in an insane world requires strength. To battle through these tidal waves of feelings which exist in the body as much as the mind. Running ideas keep cropping up and disappearing as my voices sabotage the penetrating thoughts.

To live in a world of normality would be stranger. Is it something I want or do, l live and thrive with the devil. Some people will never live to see this other side. To be balancing on the tight rope. To own up to my feelings, I think l should be depressed, I should be suffering. This racing mind stomps on my bad feelings but instead of stopping the, it argues with them and release evil venom. I want to sleep, to turn off all sound, turn off all feelings, and turn off all moods. But l want to create, let my mind wander, explore and experiment. Fighting the voices in a battle neither will ever win. I have sat silently and spilled out my thoughts. Pen and paper are my one true friend, a source of escape and a chance to be honest with my mind. Voices are everywhere, sounds are everywhere, unreal people are everywhere. Beating me down, down into hell. I'm drowning in anempty world with devils dancing in my head, dancing on my grave whilst I'm still alive.

This piece was written whilst l was changing anti-psychotic medication. I was seriously ill for two weeks after and was nearly admitted to hospital but fortunately I was able to stay under crisis team. My mum and dad were amazing as it felt as though I was being dragged though hell. As were my core-coordinator and crisis team. I never want to go through that again!

QUESTIONS

Do your ever feel like how can you trust a life where everything false? Where voices and sounds appear in silent rooms? Where strange smells wake you up even if you are fast asleep. Or when objects turn into a creature, grow legs and walk away? Do ever feel that your life is on the wrong path and that somewhere along the way you lost the concept of living? That your soul has been damaged and needs a transplant? I do!

VOICES AND PSYCHOSIS, ANOTHER SIDE TO MY WEATHER

Unfortunately, as well as my weather rollercoaster I have traits of psychotic symptoms as well. These have become more apparent when my moods are stable, appearing despite any infections of clouds or sun. Although I have used the weather to explain my moods, my psychotic symptoms are much more a part of me than the weather. I find them hard to define, hard to separate as they have always been around.

I am currently going though the process of accepting my mental illness, but, moreover these psychotic traits. Today has been hard with my voices playing up and causing me to have several break downs. Naturally I turn to writing; to let it all out, let it escape from my mind, from the voices mind.

I hear both inner and outside voices. My inner voices have a completely different meaning and an entirely unique set of beliefs then the outside voices. They are a whole different problem and are with me in my head 24/7. Everyone has one inner voice: their thinking voice, their reading voice. I, however have more, multiple in fact. They talk amongst themselves, talk to me and seem as if they take control. At night when I lie down to get to sleep my thoughts start flowing like anyone else. This is when my inner voices are at their worst.

INNER VOICES - MULTIPLE

Do you ever hear multiple voices inside your head that do not allow you to think things? You are not allowed to process things that have gone on around you, or within you. Even if you want to, you are not allowed.

The voices or 'people' in your head stop you from thinking on the inside and from talking on the outside. If you try to think about a particular subject they can stop you by creating body ticks or making you sick. They can take control completely by stopping your thoughts or conversations with your natural inner voice. Putting a hold on anything you want to think about, good or bad, they take control. This means you are not able to think or to process information which you really want to. You have no control. I can result in dissociation and/or a trip to A&E. You are totally unaware of how you have ended up there; all you wanted to do was think about your day. It was not allowed and this is the result. However, these voices are not all bad they can be nice, kind even. They can talk to you and joke making light of a situation, speaking comforting words to you. They may turn the conversation around in your head lovingly, allowing you to talk about something else. Sometimes they deliver a running commentary of your life, this maybe in short sentences which are quite easy to deal with. I suppose deep down I know they are not normal, not everyone has multiple voices, plus an inner voice. I think I think they are there to protect me. However, I am starting to feel my inner voices are a survival technique gone wrong and they are never going to go.

OUTSIDE VOICES - MULTIPLE

In contrast not only do I have inner voices, I have outside ones too. Most people have heard of people experiencing outside voices, with schizophrenia being well documented. The outside voice sound like real people, I hear three; two men and a female most the day. They chant, they sing, they abuse me but can also be rather funny. The can be completely soul destroying but at the same time I know they are not real and are a symptom of my mental illness. I know that medication makes them better. In fact I know that on the high dose of Risperdone it can cause them to disappear completely. I am sometimes able to argue back, fight them, or engorge them if I am strong enough that day. Hard to admit but if they were to go I think I would actually be lonely. They are a bit like a twin sister who is always hanging around

LIVING WITH BOTH

A wise song once had the lyrics –

'The drugs make you sane, but they don't make you better.'

This line could not have more meaning to me at the moment. Whilst I have swapped over antipsychotics medication the outside voices have got worse. But yes this is to be expected and will probably improve as the new drug work their way into my system. The problem is, the inner voices have also got a lot worse to. Are these also to do with the antipsychotics? Or are these to do with the things I am now starting to face and admit. I think there needs to be a little more knowledge and understanding on the inner voices which I experience. I feel that hearing both can be more damaging as I am unable to accept them separately.

Writing this book has helped me realise some things about the moods, voices and many of my symptoms. Unfortunately, one of my diagnoses is multiple personality disorder. I found this hard to accept, as I do not have multiple personality in the unwell sense, or in the public understanding. I may have different inner voices and voices outside my head, but I am one person. However, these voices conjour up video memories, hallucinations and smells making me disconnect from time and space. Consequently, they do cause my life to be extremely unstable and often make me do things that are out of my control. I do now accept my diagnosis

Milly Jones

This is not your home!

I imagine you think that this is your home
You like where you live
You don't want to move on

Despite the pushing of some invisible forces
You're determined to stay
And make your presence known

You bitch and complain about all of your surroundings
Giving a running commentary aloud
There is no need to be silent

You find something wrong about where you live
Picking up on every imperfection
Digging up under every seat

Instead of rebuilding and making it home sweet home
You become the house's worst tenant
As you destroy what is formed

You knock away at this place you think you own
Making holes from the cracks
Where the raindrops can fall

You say no one wants me, that I am a waste of space
That I don't deserve help from anyone
Which makes me lose my faith

You can illiterate everything so well that it's hard not to hear
To all those horrible rhyming words
And those thoughts you make real

You bitch and chant on all of my weaknesses
Making my life near impossible
But I try not to listen

But When I do I make mistakes
It's my home I'm destroying
Your just voices from my head

This is not your home that you're trying to destroy
You are the weakness
Im afraid you have to go

You are not true, you are not real
People are making me strong
Despite what you feel

That invisible force that's driving you away
Are simple, two little blue pills
Which I take everyday

Although you think that this is your home
You better start packing
You are just voices which don't belong

Self-Harm and I

This is a poem I wrote at 2 am this morning after returning from A&E.
I love writing poems at the moment even though I am not brilliant. It's
about reason why I self harm and actually gave me a surprise when I
wrote it by seeing why it had happened. Writing is helping me to start to
understand my actions and my life.

I self harmed again tonight
I am I trying understand why
My mind took control of me
I cannot tell a lie

Somehow I ended up A&E again
Luckily I was not judged

Milly Jones

I did not do it for attention
I did not do it for blood

It a funny thing this self harming lark
I guess I don't know why
I can't understand how you cutting yourself
Can make you feel so alive

For me I know I am different
I am not always the same
I go through stages of normality
Which is then broken by the pain

Imagine this, just be me for a while
Try and face my fears
I wouldn't wish this on anyone
Its not something I like to hear

My body makes me sick
Continuing throughout the day
Thoughts and voices are out of my control
Making me think a certain way

I cannot sleep straight through the night
And the nightmares take their toll
My medication is always changing
And unfortunately it shows

I have seizures which are physical
Body pains for no reason at all
My voice makes random noises sometimes
With my body there is no control

I cannot stop any of this from happening
It is all out of my hand
I have no power over my body
Makes me wonder why I am even alive

So sometimes I crack
Maybe for a few weeks
I turn this unbearable pain physical
In need of some release

Yes it may be unhealthy
Yes it may be grim
I may need emergency help
But you can judge from within

For a minute in time I have control
I am starting to understand why
Creating my own pain for once
Unfortunately builds a mini high

When things are as unstable as all this
Pain regains control
I can finally grab some power over myself
But regrettably it shows

My scars are my battle wounds
Which I am creating all the time
But I guess what I am trying to say
Is everyone deserves a life

This coping strategy I have learnt
Has developed from a child
I do not enjoy doing this to myself
But it's been going on for a while

I guess it doesn't matter how you cope
As long as you survive
My way maybe different to most
But I'm I am battling to stay alive

Milly Jones

So please excuse my arms and I
As I am try to understand
Cutting isn't always my choice
But with help I am starting to see why

CONCLUSION OF SYMPTOMS

Due to my psychotic symptoms my care-coordinator and support worker often say, sometimes you are not in control and you cannot help the times this happens. I am not saying I am not taking responsibility for myself or my life, but it is hard handling all these symptoms. So sometimes, my coping mechanisms are out of my control; from the inner voices to the outer voices, from self harm to conversion disorder. However, I know I need to accept everything on the road to recovery, but at the moment I feel I am taking one step forward and two steps back.

This chapter of writing has helped me realize how much I cope with on a daily basis and also how much I have been through. In a strange way I strongly believe that everyone is going though the same: same symptoms. That everyone hears inner voices and outside voices, have moods that destroy their life, see hallucinations all in which they have no control: their thoughts, their actions. But this is simply not true.

Although it does not bother me as much anymore, I know I am different, it is still hard to accept. Yes the drugs do make me saner, but they definitely don't make me better, not sure if I ever will be. Acceptance is the first part of recovery right? However, acceptance is a multi layered word; accepting your ill, accepting your symptoms, accepting this is your life and things might never go away. But more importantly accepting that you are different. That I am allowed to find everything a lot to deal with, and harder to cope with, because not everyone experiences the symptoms, the voice and moods in which I do. Unfortunately, I find it hard to discus my problems with the people that are there to help, mainly because I believe I am being self pitying. I think I am being rude, taking up their time which such unimportant problems which everyone else has to deal with and manage every day. Yet in fact this is not true. The reaction on my blog on Facebook it has helped show me that not everyone has these symptoms, this life. In fact, I think I am quite rare. Asking and needing help should be nothing to be ashamed of because my life is not as simple as it should be. Everyone has their own problems to deal with; mine I have to share between various people on the inside and outside just to get through the day. No wonder I am not allowed to think about things all the time, I think I would explode. Its no wonder my moods go haywire with the hallucinations and lack of sleep. I think I am starting to control all of this, but I will always be different, I will always be unique.

MOVING ON NOVEMBER 2013

Life is always complicated. I can never simply choose a path that I want to go down and follow it like the yellow brick road. Instead I am forced to choose a path that bends and turns into dark cold places and unearths some terrible feelings. Maybe that's the way of recovering from a mental illness, when you have seen and felt things only reserved for people in nightmares. Some of my book is focusing on recovery and the rocky road that it is. This is no different, as although I am making small steps they are only little progressions in what I believe is going to be a life long battle. Not just of my mental illness, but of trying to find my path to go down.

The biggest turning step I have taken at the moment is to try and regain control of my life by putting on hold my Open University Psychology degree. Through lots of discussion, and tears, I decided that I needed to take time out and fix myself. To do this successfully I need to limit the amount of stress and for once focus on my health. I have not just found this difficult I discovered it is not as simple as it seems. I have not dropped out of the Psychology course, as I have 16 years to complete, I have instead put it on hold

My feelings are that I would like to try and regain my life from where it was distorted. I am hopefully going to reapply to the Occupational Therapy degree course again for September 2014. I do not want this ill state of existence to take hold of my life any more and I want to rejoin society. Be back to my old self, the person who was taken away from me in the night. So to help achieve this, I am going to start volunteering at my local mental health centre. This should build my confidence and get me back into the working environment. I am trying my very best to make this dream a reality but it's hard. It's hard when you think so little of yourself.

When around every turn you have to teach yourself new ways to cope and be normal. When you hate yourself and what your life has become.

I want more then anything to stay stable and am fighting so much to regain control and a normal life. I am currently questioning where the separation of the Bipolar and Conversation disorder starts and ends. Where am I supposed to be placing this normal life? How am I to accept my diagnosis and move forwards with it?

My biggest battle is l have this fight of a fight going on. That I am fighting to get well and be normal but underlying l am fighting a much bigger fight, the urge not to give up. The feelings caught up in this fight are so strong and powerful it's like my whole life feels like a failure and I feel so false.

However, I am going to push these feelings aside and carry on. I have put on hold Open University and am trying my best to achieve success in this normal world. Yet my reality of normal life is such a blur that I don't know what I am aiming for. Its like my life has been tinted by a monster. I am unsure of what things to accept and take with me as baggage, and what things to throw away never to be felt again. I want to go back to OT so badly but I need a straight path l can follow. One where I believe in myself so that each day can stop being a struggle and I can help others: One where I can forget my past and accept new beginnings and in turn a new me, or maybe even the old me.

OUT OF THE OLD AND
INTO THE NEW

As always I am going to throw in a positive note. I often hear very wise words from my care coordination and support workers telling me to accept my symptoms and keep moving forwards. This is what this book and I am trying to do. I put my writing out there publicly to help others but really it is also my saviour and I am not embarrassed. I think determining the difference between the inner voices and outside voices is so important. But also, determining what is I and what are my symptoms is equally important. Many professionals get this confused and start treating you as an illness, instead of a human with difficulties. For example, my psychiatrist once asked if I was a paranoid person. I answered no, and me as a person I am not. However, if he asked if I had paranoid symptoms then the answer would have been yes. This dilemma is covered in another chapter, but I feel it is important to make whilst discussing my symptoms as it illustrates how complex it all is.

EVENTS

In February 2014, my life was to be turned upside down again but to begin with, it was not to do with me. My parents and I went on a brilliant holiday skiing in Austin. Unfortunately, I was unable to ski everyday due to feeling so low for a few days, so instead I went for walks in the snow with my mp3 player on. We all enjoyed our time there, but little did we know what was in store when we got back.

A few days after our return, my dad was laid in bed and got a pain in his chest. It was his right arm that hurt and he had begun to get shooting pains but he thought little of it. However, we all decided it was best for him to visit the doctors. The next day, our doctor phoned him saying he had to go straight to A&E. The doctor came round to our house and the ambulance came quickly afterwards. Everything was happening so fast and I was a little scared. However, my dad on the other hand remained calm. Calm enough in fact to ask if he could eat his cheese and biscuits before he was going to hospital. So as we all sat the waiting for the ambulance (a paramedic car showed up first) my dad ate his dinner.

Apparently he had had a heart attack in the night and his arteries were blocked. He stayed in hospital for a week after that and had heart surgery to put two stents in his pulmonary artery. Our world was being rocked without him at home, but my mum and I tried to carry on as normal, making sure we managed to visit him every night but also spending time to walk Jessie. He made a full recovery after two weeks in hospital in total, although now more sensitive to pains in his chest.

In the middle of all this, I attended an outpatients psychiatrist appointment with my care coordinator. I was not nervous about the appointment and was only expecting him to review my medication and change my Quetiapine to another antipsychotics. All relatively straight forwards, but little did I know what was about to happen would change my path yet again.

The doctor began like always, discussing my moods and how I had been. I mentioned about the crisis team and about finding it difficult to sleep on this new medication. I explained that I did not feel it was working and would like to change. So he agreed and swapped me to aripiprazole with details of how to reduce the Quetiapine and start the new meds. He was happy to leave me on Lithium agreeing that this medication was helping my mood.

Then, he said something that surprised not only me, but also my care coordinator too. He decided to change my diagnosis. He explained that he had read though my notes of being with EIT and my old CMHT team and felt that a personality disorder diagnosis would be more appropriate. He explained that it fit with the conversion disorder and that this diagnosis was considered less dangerous then epilepsy or bipolar. I was shocked. I didn't expect it. I knew that it had been chasing me all my life, but I thought I was on the right track with the meds and the bipolar diagnosis. I burst into tears and could not handle it.

Unfortunately, I could not get the words out of how I felt about the situation and left as a bubbling wreck. My world felt like it had been torn apart because my new diagnosis compounded my fears.

I believed that everything that happened to me was my fault. That I was causing my own problems, my own systems and that it is all down to me. I cannot understand how a happy child growing up can have such difficulties in late life to even function. Unfortunately, I have now been given two diagnosis that fuel this thought pattern and these voices. When the Doctor changed my diagnoses it changed my whole belief system. It seemed like they were taking a condition that was supposedly out of my control and handing it back into my control. I now have two diagnoses of mixed personality disorder and conversion disorder which seem to be in my hands. I have become upset at each appointment because I have been given these diagnoses and have never got to explain why. This time things would be different and I sent a letter to my Psychiatrist to explain why this new diagnosis was so upsetting.

LETTER TO PSYCHIATRIST- WRITTEN 2ND MARCH 2014

As with many people with mental health problems, I find psychiatry appointments hard. This one was particularly difficult with my dad being in hospital with a heart attack and with the recent discharge from Neuropsychological. Unfortunately, I felt the psychiatrist didn't let me explain my point of view and I got upset in the appointment. As a result I wrote and sent off this letter a week later. I got confirmation off staff at the Mental Health Society and off my Care-coordinator to send it. Basically it explains my feeling towards scientific mental health problems and psychological ones. For some reason a couple of psychiatrists kept diagnosing me with mixed personality disorder instead of bipolar. Personally, I think I have one personality and different moods so I am sticking with the original diagnosis of Bipolar. It's my life, and it explains it best, even if that is not the diagnosis on paper.

Dear Doctor,

I am writing to you to express my feelings regarding a recent appointment with yourself. I attended an outpatient's clinic a few weeks ago and became distressed during our appointment. I am taking my time to write this letter, not to disagree with the outcome of the appointment, more so to express my feelings which I was unable to do at the time. I feel this is important as I believe there were crossed opinions on what was said and how I felt.

Firstly may I start by summing up what happened? Last year you diagnosed me with bipolar disorder, after a transfer from my previous

CCTT. I have been on Lithium that has been a success, and are now changing around my antipsychotics. At the recent appointment you re-evaluated my situation and decided that a diagnosis change to a personality disorder may be more suitable. I understand how closely linked the two diagnoses are and how changes between the two are rather common. I would like to make clear that I do not disagree with the diagnosis and have always accepted that I have traits of a personality disorder. However, I will admit I was shocked at the change, as the diagnosis has chased me all my life, although professionals have always changed their mind. Nevertheless, I feel that I was misunderstood to my reaction and I would like to explain why.

I am a science girl. I like facts and figures and seeing where something has gone wrong by evidence. I have worked in pathology and researched in medical issues where there is a biological or mechanical reason for given symptoms. When the body goes wrong, I find it a lot easier to understand, learn and accept the problems if science can show what has gone wrong and why this has caused the given symptoms. This is how I work and unfortunately I feel that I am criticised for this view from my health care professionals. I know that conversion disorder is less of a major health problem then epilepsy. I also know that a personality disorder is considered a less major mental problem then bipolar. I accept this and I do not want a major health problem. However, I do have problems with my mental health and conversely my physical health. No matter if a professional considers diagnosis as less serious and or a better diagnosis; I still have the same symptoms. Again, I am not arguing the diagnostic name, as to me I am still going to have the same issues whatever the diagnosis and I won't let it change my plans. I am more trying to express that during my appointment I became upset and distressed because I have now been given two diagnoses which I find harder to grasp. I do not want the major disorders or illnesses in any way but I feel you misunderstood where I was coming from. You seemed to imply that I should be happy of the diagnosis I have because they are less major, but if you take it from my view and the way that I understand is scientific then these diagnoses take away my science process. I am happy they are considered less major, however I find them harder to understand and process which when in appointments shocks me that this appears to come over wrong to professionals.

I want to reiterate that I do not disagree with any diagnosis that I have received in the past year. However I think it is fair to send this letter to express how diagnoses are not as simple as they seem. It is not always the impact or symptoms of any diagnosis that people struggle with, however the understanding and theory behind them can be just as important. I do feel that I am criticised for this view but often I am unable to express it and that creates crossed views.

Overall, I am not concerned what cluster my symptoms are going under because it does not change my future or present plans. My care coordinator and I know what we need to work on and have a plan to help me manage my symptoms and carry on with my life. No recent events are going to change anything and in turn they will not change me. Unfortunately I did get upset at the recent appointment and didn't get to express some of my feelings. Nevertheless I was able to go home and process everything, that in turn helped me decide to write this letter. I hope you don't mind me sending this letter but I feel it's important as I find appointments hard and never quite get to say what I feel. I look forward to seeing you in June and hopefully we can discuss some of our thoughts further.

Thank you for taking your time to read this,

Kind Regards,
Milly Jones

Snippet in my mind – Moods or personality?

Express with words is what I always try and do
But sometimes they are different it depends on the point of view

Am I one person, two, three or four
Or am I the same person with moods I just engorge

Months, weeks, days go by with me just standing there
Everything seems to happen but my soul just doesn't care

I don't want to be ill, I want to take control
But something comes over me, my inner voice as a patrol

I don't understand how I feel, or what it all really means
Yesterday I was different, is that wrong or just unique

So I will try, try and try some more,
To explain my life and get a cure

Mixed Personality Disorder and Conversion Disorder

Just a few questions
I am writing this because I am confused and have some questions:
Do you ever get lots of contradictory voices in your head so that it hurts?
Do you ever feel happy but a part of you is in so much pain?

Do you ever have things jump around inside you wanting to get out?
Do you ever have such strong feelings in your body that they feel like different people?
Do you ever not have control of your own body?

That emotions make you physically tick and sick?
Do you ever have illness that appears for weeks at a time then disappears?
Is your body unstable-high blood pressure one week, low the next.

Do you forget time?
Are you unable to remember parts of your past?
Forget beyond normal?

Do you recognise people you don't know?
Do fail to recognise people you do know?

Do you have multiple inner voices?
Do they control you?
Do they argue with you?
Do they not let you think or remember things?

Do you hear voices on the outside of your head?
Do you see people who aren't there?
Do you hallucinate on a daily basis?
See patterns and things move?
Are you thrown back into memories as if they are real?

Does this cause emotional and psychical pain?
Can you see things from films in everyday life at random?
Do you get random quotes repeating and flashing around in your head?

Do you have triggers?
Do you revert back into being a child?
Do you dissociate?
Disconnect from time and space?

Do you cry for no reason at all but only realise it's happening half way though?
Do you get severe pains in your body for no reason at all?

Are you terrified to go to sleep at night because of the pain?
Do you have nightmares every night?
Do you control your dreams by lucid dreaming every night, unable to get a proper rest?
Dose emotional stress make you sick even when your asleep?
Do you ever have such vivid dreams you're not sure what's reality?

Do you convert emotional pain into physical?
Have unexplained seizures, sickness, ticks, voice problems on a daily basis?
Do you lose your voice for no reason at all?
Unable to talk inside or out, or speak in English?
Can you sometimes not understand the English language?

Do you self harm just to get control over your body?
Have you ever looked at a bandage on your arm and wonder what's under it?
Do you ever find writing or drawings that you have no recollection of doing?

Do you hate that people like you?
Are you scared to be loved?

Scared to be touched?
Do you find it hard to find a reason to live?
Feel so lonely even though there are so many people around?
But do you have the strength of a hundred men to carry on?
Do you put up with all this?

This is me. My life. Everyday is a yes

EXPLANATION OF THE FEELING INSIDE - WRITTEN AT TIME OF WRITING

Do you ever get the feeling that someone or something is inside your body wanting to get out? You don't know what it is or how to deal with it but it makes you feel odd and you can literally feel it wanting to escape. Unfortunately, I have more than one of these feelings that takes control and makes me behave in strange ways. There is a jumping one that makes me nauseous and psychically sick. It cries out random noises, so it can be heard but does not make sense. I feel like it is trying to tell me something but can't communicate normally. I can feel it jumping around inside, bouncing off my organs and trying to escape. I am not crazy, I know it's not a person but it's a bunch of feelings within me.

Another confusing bunch of feelings that I experience is that parts of my insides are trying to go on bear hunt, trying to uncover unknown things. For example, today I am ticking away, unable to stop because they want to tell me something but can't. It feels like people are digging in my mind and brain, trying to open locked cases without a key. I have no headache just a fuzzy head and an inability to keep thinking straight. Although I am managing to write, my brain and insides hurt, as these feelings are trying to escape.

These episodes are bunches of feelings built up which change how I act, making me do things like: have seizure, vomit, affect my voice and communication, make me tick and dissociate. If these feelings are so big, so strong and make such an impact on my life; how are they not different people inside of me? I know they are not different personalities but different innate bodies.

I can go through weeks of having serious stomach problems, to it then completely disappearing overnight. I will then have a killer headache for weeks for it again to disappear overnight. The strange thing is, I have about five or six medical issues, which only happen for a few weeks, then disappear. But what is more bothering is each symptom will then reappear again once the other has settles down.

DBT AND NEW BEGINNINGS

So, June 2014 brought new beginnings, new hope to my ever-increasing darkness. I began seeing Sarah, a qualified DBT therapist on Thursday June 12th 2014. She expressed such an understanding of my struggle and my need to self harm and express my feelings through my body. Everything that I said she seemed to understand and accept. I illustrate that I disagreed with the diagnosis of borderline personality disorder but that I was happy to work with her though my issues so that I could gain a life worth living.

Borderline diagnosis- I can see here that things are getting a little confused over this. I did right to the psychiatrist saying that I didn't necessarily disagree but the more I read up on it the more I came to the conclusion I have traits not the disorder.

Here we go, let's let rip
Let our world's loosen its grip

Let be free, lets not hide
Lets say everything that's inside

I'll be honest, update you all
Into my world, into my flaws

My world has changed, turned upside down
Due a diagnosis, spinning me around

It's made me embarrassed, made me ashamed
It has made me not want to live the life I have gained

They say I have conversion disorder, are mentally ill,
And that my personality is flawed as well

Apparently I am mixed a combination of two
Two cracks in my soul, two cracks in my will

My thoughts and feelings are out of control
They need restraining so that I don't cause harm

Medication won't help to seal the gaps
So it's back to therapy, to give me a chance

A chance to live, a chance to be normal
A chance to be set free and live like people

DBT, the name of the game
Twice a week, despite the pain

One whole year, two weekly meetings
It's going to be hard to discover my feelings

But I will build a new life, gain a new purpose
And I will make it through the rollercoaster circus

Currently its hard, existing like this
I am glad I have been given a chance to wish

To wish for a belief, to create a life
To get rid of the physical pain I keep entrapped

So that's me, set and saved,
On the path of therapy, for the life I have gained

It's going to be hard, it going to difficult
But I will give it my all and hope for a miracle

SO WHAT IS DBT??

DBT stands for Dialectical Behaviour Therapy. It is a yearlong intensive therapy designed to help people over come damaging behaviours and unhelpful coping strategies. The therapy consists of one group session on a Tuesday and a one to one session on the Thursday morning with a therapist. It is hoped that by learning skills and starting to recognise emotions, that bad coping skills, such as self harm will start to fade away, by being replaced with new and better coping skills. In a sense the therapy is rewiring the pathways in my brain to help form new and improved ways to deal with life and situations that I find difficult.

DBT was a new start for me and I threw myself into it with open arms. I never missed a session even when things started to go wrong, yet again.

HOSPITAL - NEUROLOGY WARD

DBT started to fix my mind and things seemed to be getting a little back on track. It was more like learning to ride a bike for the first time with stabilizers and my dad holding me tight. However, as my mind started to heal, my body started to fail, yet again

I began having strange symptoms along with my seizures and vomiting. For two weeks in august I had a stammer. I couldn't say anything properly and was hard to understand. The more I became stressed about the situation the harder and worse it became. Also during this stage my eyesight became worse and I was prescribed glasses. The sun seemed so strong and powerful that i could not see outside. I had special tinted glasses made for me so that I could see well again.

Although I had all this going on, I now look back with pride that I carried on. I managed to carry on running the clay class with my mental health cafe, attend all DBT therapy sessions, see my care coordinator, my friends and go out in public. I was pretty much a superhero at the time, if I do say so myself.

So, life was pretty rubbish and again my health was getting in the way. So I booked another appointment with the neurologist at my local hospital. He is a nice doctor and always does the best for me but what he did was a surprise. I went to see him in September and by October I was in hospital. That's right, he placed me in hospital for my symptoms.

I was in an inpatient for exactly one week on the neurology ward. My doctor explained that he didn't think he was going to find anything but he wanted to be sure and to reassure me. I had an MRI, an eye test and a three day ECG to see if I was epileptic or even had signs of MS. Amazingly I managed to attend my DBT group session with electrodes stuck to my head looking very attractive! Fortunately, he said all the tests came back clear and it was once again confirmed I had conversion disorder.

Still to this day new symptoms' scare me, so I don't feel any guilt about going for the tests although I did at the time. It was like I had my own little mental health bed in the neurology ward. I broke down numerous occasions and needed a lot of help. The thing with conversion disorder is it is always trying to trick you. It is your subconscious mind that gives you the terrible symptoms. The more you stress over them the worse you become. The neurologist was trying to prove to me that there was no real cause for my symptoms by running the tests. This did the trick and my stammer disappeared although I was still having the seizures.

Things started to get better after hospital as DBT got into its flow. My self-harrm was getting less and so were my seizures. In DBT you do a module in mindfulness this helps you stay in the present moment instead of worrying about past or future. Its rather hard to do with voices and thoughts trying to take control but once you get the hang of it its brilliant. It allowed me to focus on the present moment in turn trying to stop my seizures. I was enjoying DBT and here is a poem expressing how DBT was helping me

I am an empty tree silhouette in the sky
Something has taken over me and my life
The leaves have now vanished and I am not in sight
I am just an empty tree on a mountain up high

I can't feel the breeze as it passes me by
my world has become dark and I don't know why
The energy it takes to want to live
Has started to make me feel physically sick.

I feel like there is string attached to my heart
That there is someone there pulling it apart
That my thoughts and feelings are out of control
And that I want the ground to swallow me whole

But today I took a walk, down by the sea

To clear my head and think mindfully
I used my techniques learnt in DBT
And started to think differently

I concentrated on my feet upon on the ground
And listened to the wind as it howled all around
I could feel the freshness of the sea air
And breathe in a breath accepting it was there

My mind started wandering, but I brought it back
Back to appreciating the world and what was about
I walked in the moment and observed what was there
Both in my feelings and in the air

I noticed an urge to disappear into the sea
But I surfed the urge and accepted mindfully
That this activity is a distraction technique
Which is improving the moment and the life that I lead

When I become distressed and the bad thoughts come again
I will imagine this moment and count my breaths
In slow motion I will make myself a cup of tea
Grab some chocolate and soothe the inner me

For I am not a tree that is all alone
I have strong roots and I'm starting to grow
With the care I'm being given and lessons I'm learning
I'm starting to accept that life might have a meaning

THE BIG MOVE

In September 2014 things seemed to be looking up for me. I seemed to be gaining control back from my conversion symptoms and my self harm was less often.

I must point out at this point that my self harming had become rather severe. I would often end up in A&E needing stitches. In total I was there at least once a month to be stitched up and sent back on my way. But this wasn't going to stop me trying to live my life.

Life was looking pretty good. I had accustomed myself to walking everywhere since I was still unable to drive. This would often mean walking to my local mental health cafe half an hour away. I was still a volunteer here, running clay classes and cooking class for people like me. We all used to get on so well and I could see the OT inside me emerging again. I loved being at this cafe and always had a brilliant time, so much so I didn't want to go home.

Home began to be somewhere I sadly dreaded. My parents were being perfect but it was the environment that was the issue. It left me feeling alone and sad, increasing my urge to self harm. I tried changing bedrooms with no avail so had to look into something completely foreign to me. Supportive housing.

The whole process of trying to find somewhere seemed very complex to me, however I had one meeting with Help Direct at the my local mental health cafe and life seemed to fall into place. There was some supportive housing just up the road from me. It was ironically own by the same people who own the cafe, so seemed the perfect place to go start my new life. As I said before I am a determined person so I wasn't going to let my mental health issues get in the way. Supportive housing seemed a great way to go, this place in particular sounded great. It was staffed 24/7 with waking night staff and three staff on during the day. The place had its own flats with a communal area downstairs and an office for staff. The expectations were that you lived there for a year to eighteen months before moving on to independent living.

So I went to look around the flats the day after with my favourite support worker. The staff that were on that day were so friendly and down to earth that it made a very stressful day much more easy. I instantly warmed to the place and was shown around two flats. They were huge with their own kitchens, bathroom, bedroom and lounge. The place was furnished and decorated well. I went downstairs to discuss the possibility of moving in and they offered me a place. I was so shocked and grateful that I was on the phone that afternoon organising the move. It took about two weeks in total before I moved but it was all very exciting. I moved into flat 8.

My new home, my new beginning.

A poem – Remember

Lets start to live
Lets not hide
Let's accept the help it doesn't hurt your pride

Don't listen to the voices
Don't listen to the thought
Don't listen to anything that's out of your control

Be happy that you're here
Be happy you're alive
Be happy that you can say you're going to survive

You've made it this far
Made it though the pain
You've made it through the sun even though the rain

Milly Jones

Bad days will come
But you have got to let them go
Let them ebb away and go with the flow

You are more than you think
More than you're worth
One day you will become someone's world

Although you don't know it
You become a success
Despite what is going on in your head

Learn to live
Learn to love life
This is the only way that you will survive

The 100% that you hate your self
Turn it around into something else

Become your own friend
Become your own partner
Become someone that you love, without all the drama

You are here, you are alive
You derserve all this,
There is no need to hide

So when you're feeling down
Read this to yourself
And remember it was you not someone else

LIFE IN SUPPORTIVE HOUSING

I moved into new flat, my new home on 5ᵗʰ of September 2014. Flat eight was all mine and it was large but comfortable. It took me two days to move in completely, getting everything unpacked and sorted. Luckily, I still had some kitchen things packed up from university so didn't need to buy much more for my new adventure.

Everything seemed to be going to plan and the first few weeks flew by. I was catching the bus to DBT on a twice-weekly bases and still running my ceramic classes at the mental health cafe. Tuesday is DBT session now took 2 and half hours on a bus to get to. I would set off at ten for a one o'clock meeting. This meant walking from the local hospital to the place where it was held, which took about half hour. I didn't mind though. I was still keen on DBT and loved listening to my music singing along to Joseph and his Technicolor dream coat sound track on the way.

Things at the flat were great for the first two months. I made a new friend and we loved playing games together. However, I was still struggling quite badly. Mental illness never seems to leave you alone even when you are trying your best to move on. My now new life wasn't turning out to be the recovery plan that I wanted. I thought that if I changed my surroundings then this would help change my situation. It did not.

Unfortunately, my mood rollercoaster decided to pay another visit. Luckily, I wasn't having the days of getting burnt by the sun, but instead I was being showered by rain and storms that no one would wish to encounter. I began dissociating pretty bad and would lose clumps of time coming around in the office holding an elephant teddy named Nelly. The staffs were wonderful with me, supporting me when I came round. It was so bizarre. The thing with my symptoms and dissociate episodes is they seem to happen the more I become relaxed. When I'm of normal mood and relaxed I am guaranteed that I will have some sort of episode to spoil the moment.

> *Here is where I have to admit my symptoms make me feel like I am being punished for something I did, said or thought. I'm unsure what I have ever done wrong but I'm guessing it was something bad.*

So my life was ticking b quite quickly in my new home, what with the missing gaps in time and spending evenings playing games. I loved the freedom I was gaining living independently and filled most of my time with craft work and baking. As I said before, my moods where starting to become a rollercoaster ride again. I was switching into deep dark depressions then back again. The staff at my home didn't agree with the diagnosis, instead treating me however I presented that day. This could range from happy go lucky Milly, full of the joys of spring, to dark cloud covered Milly who would sit for whole night crying and crying, hysterical.

My care coordinator kept a close eye on me over the time of the move. Since August I had been ringing her nearly every day making her a promise to stay safe untill the next time we spoke. At times she was literally keeping me alive. She visited me many times in my new flat. She loved the place and with words of encouragement spoke of how well I was doing to move out and my determination to start a new life. Kate had been my care coordinator since my move back in 2012. We got on so well and she was an amazing care coordinator. Unfortunately, in October, just one month after my move, Kate announced she was leaving. It was hard news to take and it hit me hard but I was happy for her as she seemed so excited for her new job. I wrote her this poem as a leaving gift and gave it her in a frame.

Dear Kate
How do I express
What the these two years
With you have meant

You have always been there
Through thick and thin
Through ups and downs

And tumbling winds

Together we have laughed
Together we have giggled
Sometimes I have cried
But you have always listened

You have put a smile on my face
And a tear drop in my eye
Yet you are always there
You're my miracle in disguise

You've stood by me as I have fallen apart
And I will always trust you with all my heart
You have literally kept me alive when I was alone
A promise to you gave me the will to carry on

You're more then just a care coordinator
You have become my friend
You are an amazing person
And I'm glad you were there

I am sad you are leaving
I can not tell a lie
But I'm happy you're moving on
And reprocessing your life

I know you'll do well
Within your next stage
But please never forget
The care you gave

You mean an awful lot to me
And I never forget
To this I would like to say thank you
And wish you well in your next steps

DOWN HILL STRUGGLE

After Kate left my blue skies seemed to turn very dark. Although I was struggling intensity with demons when she was around, they seemed to get much worse when she left. My dissociation episodes began getting much worse making me appear like different people. My new care coordinators was a nightmare, she was never around and I seemed to go from having a brilliant care coordinate to having no one. I was still in supportive living at this point and the staff where amazing, however, they couldn't do much for me.

I also found myself struggling with DBT at this time. Although I was hanging on in there you could tell I was finding it difficult and my symptoms where so different to others people. I felt I had no other way to express them.

Meanwhile my supportive living was for the homeless and people with mild mental health problems. It was starting to become obvious that I was more severe than housing company though. My needs were starting to become intense with the dissociation, moods and conversion symptoms. Unfortunately, in late November 2014 I got so distressed and ill that I was admitted to my local mental health hospital.

HOSPITAL

Eight years after my last admission, I was back in Underwood. I was admitted to an acute ward for adults with mental health difficulties. The first week was scary. I didn't know what to do, how to act or how to appear. It was a really frightening time, yet luckily I was so ill I can not remember most of it. I was there for a total of four weeks, inside, locked away. During the last week my mood had switched and I was back to my bubbly old self. All I remember from my low mood was listening to music over and over again and sitting in my dormitory crying. I made some good friends that admission and it happened to fall over Christmas.

Every year I used to love Christmas. Luckily before I was admitted I was able to go Christmas shopping and cut down my own Christmas tree for my flat. I had made some decoration and decorated my flat all sparkly. However, when Christmas actually came around I didn't care at all. It was like it wasn't happening at all. I ate Christmas dinner all on my own, this made me silently sad but really I wasn't bothered. Christmas wasn't Christmas this year; it was just another day,

My friends and family were amazing when I was inside; they kept visiting me and bringing chocolate, which is always good. The staff in hospital were also amazing. I got on with them all so well. They were always there when I needed them for a listening ear when I was struggling. I had some smiles, I had some tears but most of all they made me able to survive.

I was discharged on January 5th 2015. I was so happy to free: I was so happy to be alive. I had decided that I would never self-harm again and I was finally cured. I was so cured in fact that I decided to apply to university again to do Occupational Therapy for the second time round. I decided on the part time application and wrote out my personal statement.

PERSONAL STATEMENT

An Occupational Therapist's role is to empower and I am passionate about returning to OT as a career. I have experiences firsthand how the use of therapeutic activity can help give purpose to life and empower a person's self belief. Small actions can make a big difference not only to the client themselves but also to their family and friends. OT helps people directly and indirectly to achieve an independent lifestyle. Whether its through adoptions or therapeutic sessions OT can work on people's difficulties by building on their strengths and help regain their confidence. This can help give people a new lease of life and allow them to live independently.

I am currently volunteering at a rehabilitation centre where I work with individuals providing company and reassurance in their time of need. The short stay hospital provides help for a variety of patients and each individual needs to be looked at on a personal account. I enjoy this personal aspect of care and believe getting to know the client can empower their ability to keep going despite their difficulties. I have shadowed the OT at the centre and was amazed by how much impact their role made. The hospital is nurse lead and the role of the OT is very valued. As a volunteer I am able to share in their delivery of personal care and enjoy seeing clients improve in such a small length of time. l am committed to my volunteering and attend at least once a week.

I also volunteer for LUPIN that is a service user group run by a local University where I work with trainee psychologists helping to give a clients perspective to their training. I attend a varied number of groups a couple of times a month and thoroughly enjoy the personal aspect can bring to their course.

At the moment I am completing level 2 NCFE in ceramics at White Cross College. I am committed to this course and attend every week completing both practical and academic work. I have already successfully completed level 1 NCFE last year and have enjoyed the new skills I have learnt.

I have also committed to attending a confidence course with a local mental health support team where I am building up my self-esteem and confidence. At the moment I am also arranging and organising some laughter therapy sessions to be run with my bipolar group and within the mental health support cafe. I believe this will provide some fun to people in difficulty.

Since leaving OT in 2011 I have kept myself up to date with academic study through completing two Open University modules and currently working through an online diploma in CBT. I thoroughly enjoy studying and have achieved high marks in my assignments. All of my work was distant learning and I was able to organise my time and discipline myself to work. Unfortunately I am dyslexic that means reading and re-reading text is more difficult but I have found ways to overcome this and do not let it get in my way.

In my spare time I am a keen walker and fell walker. I love escaping for the day with my dog going on various walks in the Lake Distract. In the winter months, I am also a keen skier. I try to get in at least one holiday a year travelling with friends and family. I am also a keen traveller and have travelled around India for a month with a friend and also around Northern Europe for two weeks. I organised my trips independently and hope to make it to Vietnam and Cambodia in the coming years. I love seeing different cultures and believe we can learn a lot from each other.

When I am not out and about I have taught myself to crochet and spend hours making crafts and bags. In addition to this I also make hardback books and rag rugs for family members and friends. I have a diagnosis of Bipolar disorder and have found craft to be the perfect therapeutic treatment allowing me to express and distract myself. I hope that through training to be an OT I can help others see their potential and build on the strengths they have to become successful independent individuals

BANG!

Unfortunately, as I was about to find out this positive me, this well me didn't last long. It didn't last at all.

I was soon thrown back into my rollercoaster circus. My moods, my dissociation, the conversion symptoms all hit me again like a boulder. I was smashed. Smashed into little pieces again. The crisis team came to see me most days so keep me safe and in essence keeping me alive. But, this turned out to not be enough. Unfortunately on February 2nd 2015 I, was admitted for the third time to Underwood mental health hospital. Little did I know this was by no means going to be a short stay.

UNDERWOOD TAKE THREE

I was in hospital for a total of 23 weeks, just over five months. Fortunately, I cannot remember nor want to remember the first two months of my stay. I was extremely low and extremely unwell. I have been told stories which I don't like to believe and are surprised at how I acted.

It was just after a week's admission when all I wanted to do was leave to kill myself. During my three weeks out I had attempted to take my life three times and cut myself twice requiring stitches. I had collected and stored up lots of paracetamol to take with vodka. I had a plan, I had a letter written out to my parents and I had all my funeral arrangements sorted. Fortunately, the staff members found me on each occasion at my supported living. They literally saved my life but felt I was too at risk for them to carry on caring for me. So I was admitted and sectioned at Underwood.

On February 11th 2015 I was sectioned for the first time

My first section was a Section 5.2 put on me by one of the nurses. This section can last for 4 hours in which a Doctor needs to be found to either rescind the section or resection me. I was reviewed and changed to a Section 5.4 by a doctor. This section is a doctor section for 72 hours. Ironically this nurse became my favourite nurse although I hated her at the time. My third section came 72 hours later when I was placed on a Section 2. A section 2 means that the doctor and staff can keep you in hospital for an assessment period of 28 days. I was sectioned by my own GP and an independent social worker called a AMP worker (Approved Mental Practitioner). I cannot remember much of this happening thought it was reported that I was talking about suicide as such an everyday thing. I couldn't comprehend that it was wrong in any way, as I couldn't personally see any other way forward.

One month later, I was then sectioned again on a Section 3. A section 3 means the doctor and staff can keep you in hospital for up to 6 months to give treatment such as medication. An independent doctor and social worker again came in to place this section on me. Again the memory is a blur, but suicide was still very much on my mind and my self-harm was again still severe.

In total I managed to self-harm five times requiring stitches in hospital. Looking back this is something I'm very not proud of. I feel I lied to staff and snuck things in. Overall it kind of help show how ill I was as my actions were completely out of character.

Hospital was a hard time, I was still going to DBT at the start of being admitted but unfortunately this started to fail. Although I thought I was still engaging, my therapist was finding it hard for me to carry on. I hadn't stopped self-harming and she said I was keeping one step in suicide instead of engaging with DBT fully. We carried on a few weeks in February discussing whether I was ready to carry on or if I wasn't ready for the therapy at all. It was a hard decision as I already felt like a failure in most parts of my life, but eventually it seemed best for me to leave DBT behind. I had completed 6 months of the course but this is where my adventure ended. I was sad, upset and left very alone.

Unfortunately, things weren't going to get better. Later that week I had a CPA meeting, with the doctor, my new care coordinator and staff members. It was decided by my supportive living that things weren't working out there and I needed more care then they anticipated. My mental health hit an all time low as I was forced to hand in my notice on the flat. I now had nowhere to live, no therapy and was technically homeless stuck in a section three.

THE TURN AROUND…

On March 10th 2015 Underwood closed down and patients and staff moved to a newly built mental health hospital. The place was called 'The Whales In' and was a new 154-bedded hospital to accommodate Lancashire mental health needs. I was brought to jellyfish ward which was a little strange at first. For a start they decided to build the hospital right near the M55 with a motorway bridge just a stroll away, great! The ward was nice, though very clinical. We now had our own bedrooms with ensuite facilities. I didn't like the ward at first, but there again I dislike change. Yet as the weeks ticked away I grew used to it and we had kept the same brilliant staff so that was a bonus.

The Whales In actually turned out to be my saviour. I meant one of now best friends, Amy, here. Together we quickly got known as double trouble spending our days on leave together and most of our time, laughing and sharing secrets. We were pretty much inseparable but in a good way. We kept each other strong and out of harm's way. Ironically it was Amy who first read my first draft of this book saying it should be published, and so if it is, it is all thanks to her.

My rollercoaster was still happening in hospital and my Doctor, who I found fantastic, thought it best if I was to have therapy and medication. I was still on the Lithium and antipsychotics at the time but was the need of PRN as well. PRN is prescribed when required to calm people down. Often when my rollercoaster hit and I required the use of my umbrella or sun cream I would have some PRN to calm me down. This didn't always work and I was restrained once or twice. This means holding me down till I calmed down.

So therapy and medication seemed a good way forward. I heard of a place in Yorkish. Since I now had a diagnosis of emotional unstable personality disorder this seemed like the perfect place. The new rehab center seemed amazing, treating people with similar difficulties but it is a hard place to get into. The unlocked ward was 14 bedded where you could have your own freedom and take responsibility for your own life again. The plan would be to stay there for one year doing DBT assessed therapy whilst living in a therapeutic community. The prospect of going there seemed a million miles away but I discussed it with the staff and then the doctor and it was decided they would make a referral.

In April 2015 I was given a letter by one of the support workers. I was so excited that I tore it open and to my delight it was a letter from the rehab center. I was accepted to go for a assessment on Friday 10th March 2015 at 10.30 am. I was so excited, so pleased and so nervous all at the same time. I couldn't believe somewhere as significant as there would accept me for assessment. It seemed out of this world.

THE ASSESSMENT

The night before I got no sleep whatsoever, I was sat talking and watching TV all night. Unfortunately, nerves got the better of me but luckily it was the night before not the day of my assessment. The staff where so nice making me brews and talking to me making me less anxious about the day ahead. The rehab was a three hour car journey away so I managed to get forty winks in the car journey up there. This was especially fortunate as my dad has on awful taste in music so it also made the journey much quicker.

Before I knew it we were there. The place we drove up to was amazing, it was like somewhere straight off a film. It was a beautiful old building with acres of green grass in the front and at the back, in fact all around. We parked up on a car park next to some horses in a field. It was a bright sunny day and everything looked so angelic as we headed towards the front entrance.

I was in to see the psychologist right on time at 10:30. He was a lovely man who made a great first impression on me. We seemed to have lots of things to talk about. I told him about my normal upbringing, my numerous courses I had started, all about my mental health history beginning from the start with early intervention, the voices, the moods and the self harm. The appointment quickly passed and as soon as it started it was time to finish.

I was then shown to the unit where I would be staying if I was to gain a place. The ward was so homely and comfortable with nice sofas and carpeted floors. It was a lot different to any hospital I was used to. Everyone there was so inviting and friendly. I went straight to dinner when I came on the unit and was quickly involved in the conversation going on. Eating is one of the criteria they keep an eye on in this Rehab so the food you choose is very important. I personally do not have an issue with food so found eating around others un-problematic. I enjoyed my lunch and meeting the other residents. I felt at home here and was looking forward to the afternoon.

The afternoon session came quickly around. This session involved meeting the other residents formally and them assessing me to see how I would fit in with the program. I was pretty nervous by this, knowing I had to make a good impression. To my amazement it all went really well. I was asked some basic questions about my health and my self harming behaviours but nothing too daunting. I actually found myself enjoying meeting everyone and my nerves quickly vanished. After this session my assessment was over.

As quickly and promptly as it had begun, it had finished and I found myself sat back in my dad's car by 2 pm heading back home. The whole day had been such a whirlwind of adventure that I couldn't stop smiling all the way home. I loved the place, I loved the atmosphere and i loved the people. But was I ready to put in the hard work, a year long therapy course, living away and giving up self-harm - yes I think I finally was.

So all I had to do now was sit and wait. Wait for a letter to be handed over to me saying if I was accepted or not.

10 days later it happened. One of the health care assistants handed me a brown envelope. I was terrified as I opened it and read the three page long letter. Unfortunately by the end I was smiling so much it hurt. I had been accepted. I was so happy, so pleased that life could begin. I quickly wrote a reply.

MY ACCEPTANCE LETTER

Dear Doctor and residents of the rehab programme,

Firstly, may I thank you for the opportunity to attend the assessment day on May the 8th. I thoroughly enjoyed looking around and meeting yourself and current residents. On the visit to the acorn programme I found the place extremely inviting and the grounds beautiful. Everyone was so friendly and made me feel very relaxed on a nervous day. I really appreciated this as it helped give a lovely feeling about the place, making it feel homely. Everyone at the rehab programme was approachable and helped me look forward to going.

Secondly, I would like to thank you for your detailed letter and the acceptance into your programme. I feel very grateful for this opportunity. Your letter expressed everything that we talked about and showed an understanding of my struggle.

From what I now know about the your programme I feel the course can really help me. I do not take this course of therapy on lightly and understand it's going to be extremely hard work. I believe I am now at a place in my life where I can share my secrets when in a therapeutic environment such as your programme.

Thank you very much for this opportunity,
I look forward to seeing you all shortly if, or when I gain funding,
Yours sincerely,
Milly Jones

THE WAIT..

The wait to go to this new rebah was a long and tiring one. In total it took 12 weeks from assessment to admission on 21st July. Funding was a painful process and was deled by four weeks for unforeseen circumstances. I eventually received the good news in June 2015 and received my admission date a week later.

Unfortunately, my life is never plain sailing, and my moods were up and down on my rollercoaster ride. Things hit rock bottom whilst I was waiting for funding and am admission date, the stress of it all was just too much. I hate to admit it but in the last week of June I fell short and self harmed pretty badly. So badly in-fact it needed surgery. This scared me. I had lost the feeling in my thumb and it constantly felt like pins and needles until the surgery that I had on 8th July.

The operation went pretty well although the feeling in my thumb was slow to return. In fact I still haven't got feeling completely back to this day. It scared me immensely that I was able to self harm so badly yet in hindsight and in a strange way it was good. It provided me with a reason not to self-harm again because I was starting to scare myself.

Shortly after my operation I was admitted to the new rehab. A new place, a new adventure and a new beginning.... or so I thought.

LEAVING THE HOSPITAL
AND HEADING OUT

Before I begin the rehab journey with you, I'm going to start by saying how hard it was to leave the Hospital. I had made some really good friends there, one of my best friends in fact. I didn't want to leave comforts of my surroundings or any of the staff. But on the same note, when two things are true, I love it, I was about to own my life, make it back to how it used to be. I was sad to say goodbye, but I was excited for a new beginning. I cried a lot that day as I walked out leaving the ward that had saved my life but hoping that I will never go back too.

My parents and I decided to go there the day before my admission so spent the evening and night over there, then things were not rushed. We had a lovely evening, eating out and playing cards and I was quickly getting to like this new city. It reminded me so much of my old university city, however I found this comforting and upsetting all at once.

The morning of my admission came quickly around and before I knew it, we were stuck in traffic trying to get to the retreat. My nerves were flowing and my hands were getting sweaty. Was this going to be the end of my hell?

My evergreen tree

I am an evergreen tree
I stand tall and proud
My leaves are so elegant
As I solicit the sky

Milly Jones

My thought branches are long
Beautiful yet strong
They provide me with strength
To carry on

My roots they hold me
Firm to the ground
Where I fetch my joy
In order to survive

The wind may blow
And I will shake
But my leaves hold on
With hope and faith

I am an evergreen tree
I stand proud and tall
Darkness may come
But may leaves will not fall

REHAB NUMBER 1

The rehab was a beautiful place, just outside of the city near a local University. The grounds were amazing, like something from a movie. Jessie, my dog seemed to be enjoying herself on the grass smelling out the rabbits as we unpacked the car.

When we arrived my buddy, who was another service user, and the admission doctor greeted me. I was shown to my room where I was allowed to unpack and then was taken through to sign some paperwork and documents and had a recap of why I was there. My parents left quite quickly and quite emotionally. It was really hard saying goodbye to them but I knew I was now in safe hands.

My first meeting with everyone was at dinnertime, it strange and scary. My heart was beating so fast and my palms were sweaty but everyone was lovely. I didn't say much that day and kept rather quiet with little eye contact. This was a new terrifying place with new routines and new people. Unfortunately though my gut feeling didn't like it... You should always trust your gut right!

The day:

7 -8 breakfast - Make your own - Ok I like this. Making my own drinks and breakfast - finally a little bit of independence

9 - 10 morning meeting - After the first few, I sadly really disliked this. We were given the opportunity to discuss how we were feeling and what day held

10 - 12 groups - Various groups like art or DBT or personal psychology therapy

12 - 12.30 dinner – HARD. Now I didn't have food issues but I found dinner hard. Your plate was piled high and you had to eat everything on it.

12.30 - 1 after meal support – Talk about how dinner felt and what we had eaten. Strange when I hadn't experienced food issues before

13 - 15 groups - Various groups again

16 - 17 afternoon meeting - Discussion of feelings again. Hard and I disliked this.

17 – 17:30 tea – Hard again

17:30 -18. After meal support - same as lunch

18 - check in - See how you were doing

20 - check in - See how you were doing

This routine was five days a week, of course groups under run and there was some free times but at lot was in a very strict routine. In my free time I loved going for a walk around the grounds. It was great to have my music on and to be on my own. I had attached myself to the song - Shawdowland from the Lion King. It seemed extremely fitting as most the time I was walking around, often crying.

After two weeks of being at the program, you must write an acceptance letter as a promise, this binds you to the course of treatment. I decided to write mine in a poem form.

Acceptance poem

Here at rehab I stand questioning
What my life really means
It's only the second week on my path
But things are being to sink in

Do I have the strength to carry on
To be part of life
To make something of myself
And watch that tree gain some height

Can I lead myself out of the darkness
Which is keeping me in entrapped
Accept the new path i have taken
And the choices throughout

Can I accept the care here
Which seems to come from the heart
Although it seems so foreign to me
Makes me want to fall apart

Do I want the life I have
To become a life worth living
I might be able to make something out of myself
If I start believing

Although I am a frightened little rabbit
Wanting to run for cover
I have recognised that the cover is unhelpful
There's only me that will suffer

So yes I have the strength to carry on
Yes I can accept the care that is given
Yes I do want to be led out of the darkness
And yes I do want a life worth living

All I can promise is that I will try my best
And to attend every group
I will help those who are struggling
And in turn myself ask for help

It is going to be hard
It is going to difficult
Because I have blocked out so many emotions
That untangling them will be a miracle

But wherever be this journey may lead me
Let my heart be the one to decide
As I commit myself to fight for my existence
And internally fight for a life

Unfortunately this setting of rehab was harder than I thought and I hated it. I wasn't fitting in at all. The girls were nice enough but I didn't feel like I was bonding and in all truth I felt well...well!

I convinced myself and in fact everyone there that I was mended, fixed, finished being crazy. I felt the rehab wasn't for me, I didn't need it. I thought I was wasting money and that the programme wasn't suiting me at all. All in all I hated it. So on the 28th of July just one week later I left. I was cured, I was well but actually what was I thinking...

I haven't gone into this rehab in much detail as I can't remember everything. I really didn't enjoy it there but I'm not saying it's a bad place. In fact for some people I know it works brilliantly and that's a fact but for me it didn't cover my needs.

THE STRUGGLE

By Wednesday I was at home all bouncy and free. I was so happy to be home. To be playing cards with my parents and going back to visiting my local mental health cafe. I was straight into walking my dog round new lanes and places near me. I loved that people weren't watching me and that I didn't have people writing notes on me. All in all, I loved being happy and free.

Unfortunately, this didn't last long, not long at all. Inevitably I was home for a week until the crap hit the fan so they say. On the 5th of august 2015 I took my quite a serious overdose with all the intentions to die. I really wanted to end it and cease to breathe anymore -I wanted to die. I had written out a suicide letter, incorporative plans and placed them in an envelope. I wasn't scared but more at peace, however the peace went when the lethal medication overdose caused me to be violently sick. My brain suddenly snapped into gear and decided this wasn't going to work. I wasn't somewhere away from everyone so someone would be bound to find me and I didn't want that. So I conjured up the courage to phone my friend and told her. She phoned my dad for me and I was quickly rushed off to hospital,

General hospital isn't exactly that fun when you have just tried to kill yourself. It not somewhere you exactly want to be. I felt embarrassed, ashamed, a failure, that everyone was laughing at me for failing to do it right.

Medically, I had blood taken and put on a drip to override the meds I had taken. Mentally, I didn't want any of it but my parents were there. I had to do for them.

The next week I spent in hospital, in my own room, being watched. It wasn't very nice at all but the staff were lovely. Again, medically I was doing ok but mentally I wasn't good, wasn't good at all. I was having side effects from the overdose of the antipsychotics and had increased restless legs. It made it extremely hard to sleep and that was making me feel even worse.

Fortunately, after 5 days the crisis team (mental health team) came to see me and discharged me home. No one at all was happy about this and for the first time neither was I.

I was left confused and suffering. I didn't feel I belonged anywhere, and that I wouldn't be able to keep myself safe. I didn't want to go home, or go to The Whale in, or The rehab again, but I had to do something.

Unfortunately, on the 20th August I reluctantly decided to try and go back to the rehab. This wasn't as easy as I thought. I was required to attend a meeting with both the service users and staff. In my heart I didn't want to go back at all, yet my heart was torn by my parents who were literally struggling to keep me alive. The meeting did not go well. I was bullied and abused by one patient saying I had split the group and being extremely harsh to me. None of the staff stepped in and I left in tears. That chapter of my life was definitely over. But what was going to happen now??

ORANGE HOSPITAL

The day started like any other Friday. I was feeling pretty low but coping. I walked Jessie to the mental health café and had some good chats with my friends. But the clouds kept coming in thick and fast. I was soon drowning in bad thoughts, suffocated under their weight; I left the cafe holding back the tears. I practically ran all the way home. Well, when I say ran I do not mean like Usain Bolt, I mean more like a fast walk with tears streaming down my face.

I reached my house within half an hour and struggled to place the key in the lock my eyes were watering that much. Unfortunately, I did, and went straight upstairs and....slash. The crimson blood was flowing free from my now freshly cut arm. Crap, what have I done again. The thoughts came quick and fast, but my arm kept bleeding and I kept cutting. Soon I was crippled mess on the floor and only ceased to finish when I heard my parents return. I reluctantly clean myself up and headed down stairs to appear normal and fine. But I was not. My blotchy red face and blood seeping through my arms told a different story. Soon my parents noticed and questions were fired, getting louder and louder and more concerned. I regrettably broke down again, was quickly shipped into the car and off to A&E.

Now as you have gathered A&E is not a strange place for me to be but this time felt different, as I sat getting my own arm stitched again by the doctor he was asking me the usual questions but was not getting the usual answers.

1. What has brought you here?
2. Was it on purpose?

3. Was it with Suicidal intent?
4. Do you feel Suicidal?

I stuttered and crumpled under his interrogation and next minute found myself all stitched up, lying in a bed needing go to sleep. The doctor had decided it best to keep me in so that I could see the crisis team.

The crisis team didn't arrive until the next day, in which time I had been actively telling my parents and staff how much I wanted to die and disappear. They reassured me the best they could but I was a mess. When the crisis team did finally arrive, I was told I was going into hospital and that a bed was available in Hospital 40 miles away.

Orange Hospital was about an hour and a half away from my house but I knew I had to go. I agreed to go informally. Within an hour I was a nervous wreck. Scared and terrified, I was pack into an ambulance and sent to Orange Mental Health Unit. It was scary experience as it was new and a mixed ward.

Overall I spent four weeks in there but can hardly remember things from this time. The ward was ok although there wasn't much Occupational Therapy things going on. We got to go on walks which was good but other than that it was rather glum.

Right now, it feels like yesterday being there when in fact in was over a year ago. It's funny your mind wandering back to memories.

After my time was up in Ormskirk I was discharged and happy to be free again.

DISCHARGE AND ADMISSION

Free......... Free falling more like. I was home for a total of 36 hours before my care coordinator came for her 48-hour check up. I thought things seemed to be going quite well internally, that was until I let the curtains open and my mask drop. I could be brave any longer; I couldn't keep up the act. I was drowning and needed some one to save me.

Next thing I knew I was a helpless pile of bones jumbled on the floor. I was struggling to breathe as I hung tight on the empty shell that in encased me. Things weren't good. They hadn't been for a while but I had kept up the persona that they were. Yet now, in this minute I broke down in front of my care coordinator and cried desperately for help.

This time it didn't go unnoticed and my care coordinator was quickly on the phone to the crisis team trying to find me a bed. The crisis team assessed me and put on the waiting list that luckily only took a couple of hours.

Before I knew it I was on my way to the hospital, luckily this time to The whales in, my old familiar ward and familiar staff. I was terrified and upset; I was happy and relieved. As DBT taught me, two things can be true at once. I was scared because I felt I had let all my staff down and was ashamed of walking though those doors again. But I was relieved to be going somewhere I knew. Back to people I knew, and I knew would help me.

So on the 25th of September 2015 I was admitted back to The Whales in, back to my ward and back within the mental health system. I breathed a deep breath and with tears crawling down my face I stepped onto the ward.

Milly Jones

Everyday a struggle...

Today I am really struggling
I just can't find the light
I'm being pulled two ways
The ropes becoming tight

I feel trapped in the middle
Screaming and shouting
But my silence is deafening
I can't express why I'm feeling

I want to talk
I want someone to listen
But I don't dare tell anyone
The struggle I'm experiencing

I remain silent and strong
Literate that I am fine
But inside all my tears
Are building up inside

I want to admit
The things in my head
But I don't understand them
So the words are left unsaid

My pain is so incredible
As I remain silent and strong
But inside I am dying
Why can't I just tell someone what is wrong

WINTER MONTHS IN
THE WHALES IN

I was admitted to again to hospital in the September and by the first week in October I was placed on a Section Three. Things were not going well for me; I was finding places and means to self-harm with and over all struggling with the constant thoughts to end my life. They were all coming fast and thick; however a few things happened which seemed to help in a strange way.

In early October my mum was regrettably diagnosed with Cancer. Luckily it was found quickly and was still at an operable stage. She found out due to her filling in a screening form on her sixtieth birthday. My mum means the world to me and I would class her was one of my best friends. It was hard not to be around her as she struggled to cope, however she handled it extremely well. She is a very matter of fact person my mum, so just gets on with things without a fuss.

Also in late October my Brother came home from Canada and decided to come down and pay us all a visit. It was amazing to see him and speak person to person. It made me realise how much I miss him and think that he is amazing. We had a brilliant time chatting together and I was allowed some leave to go to the cafe so allowed me time off the ward. He was only over for one week before he had to go back to Canada. But it is a week I will remember.

THE WHALES IN AND CHRISTMAS

The next few months were so wasted and blurry it's hard to remember what I was getting up to. Luckily my best friend was already on the ward which took some of the anxiety away, I quickly found her and we bonded over laughing about how pitiable our situations were. If you don't laugh you cry I guess!

The next few we months I was on and off level three (one to one observations), had leave then didn't and was on a rollercoaster of mood. Unfortunately, I have forgotten to mention that Orange Hospital had taken me off most medication including the Lithium. Their reason behind it was me being on too strong meds for my age and the fact I had overdosed on Lithium in the previous months. This decrease was not to be for the better. As the weeks went on from my first admission my mood went lower and lower. I was struggling to breath and struggling to function, I dipped into a massive depression, finding it hard to see any light. Luckily the amazing doctor there knew me, placing me back on Lithium that heightened my mood to a more settled position.

Falling...a poem from the fall

F alling down out of the sky
A bducted by pain as it arrives
L eaving me with nothing, out of control
L oneliness takes over and swallows me whole
I ngested by pain my mind has gone
N umb and lost my only home
G oing down feeling forever alone

CARRYING ON

My birthday came up in December just before Christmas. I never look forward to my birthday anymore, it's like people are celebrating my failure. Failure of surviving the last year instead of living and celebrating the fact I hadn't killed myself. Unfortunately, at 3 am on my birthday morning I was sat in A&E being stitched. Not good.

My birthday was also extremely difficult this year for a different reason. My mum got her operation date on the 3rd December, two days before my birthday. It was a hard day waiting around for news of how it went and how she was. On a positive note, they managed to remove the entire tumour and my mum was placed in ICU for only a couple of days. It was really hard to go and see her in the hospital. She had tubes coming out of her neck and various places on her body. It's not nice seeing someone you love in pain and I felt that it was hard. However, I was kept safe by the fact I could go talk to staff when I got back. I feel sorry for my dad, it must have been a lonely week doing everything and staying on his own for the weeks my mum was in hospital. They're both amazing people.

Christmas 2015 also came whilst I was in this hospital. This was to be my second Christmas in hospital. Luckily this time I had a few hours leave although I found this extremely difficult. I decided to have my Christmas dinner at hospital and go home for a few hours in the afternoon. The dinner was ok with everything a normal Christmas dinner has. I ate with two of my friends on the ward at the time and did crackers with the staff. We all got presents off the staff as well as a little treat. It was sweet and stress free but going home afterwards was hard.

I found it hard to be with my family, especially this year as everything had changed. I had nephews now who changed Christmas and my mum was still finding things hard after her operation. So everything seemed different, I enjoyed it don't get me wrong but I found it hard, ever so hard. I only had 3 hours out in total until I went back to the ward. I didn't mind because I didn't want to spoil it for myself or other people. Back on the ward, we played games and had an early night. Overall Christmas 2015 wasn't too bad but by this time next year things really need to be improved.

New Year passed and went with no fuss again. In fact I was in bed by 11, fast asleep when the bells began to chime celebrating the new incoming year. The next weeks were hard. I had now had most my leave cancelled and took a bit of a drop again. I was on level 3 for all of February until I was informed of my move.

NEW YEARS RESOLUTION

Lots of people are setting targets and trying to make sure 2016 is as good or better then 2015. Well I'm no different, although in fact it's just another day, I'm trying my hardest to reach a new level of functioning again. So to help me get out of hospital I have a plan. I am going to create a self-harm blanket. A reward blankets.

THE PLAN

Every day I don't self-harm I will sew a square pattern piece of material together. If I do (which isn't the end of the world), it is just a plain square; I will sew solid colour pieces of fabric into a line of fabric. This will create each month; a line of square pieces some plain, some pattern in a certain colour. I will then change colour each month to create strips for a blanket. My unique idea :)

During my stay on the ward a new placement was researched for me. It was decided that the a open door rehab was a unsuitable placement and instead the care coordinator and hospital team decided I needed a locked rehab. This was scary, it meant I would be going on a section and couldn't just leave, like I did previously. I was scared, nervous and excited all at the same time. As the weeks rolled on I was assessed by three different rehabs and accepted by all. We decided on a placement in Wales that seemed to meet my needs the best. In late January my funding was agreed and all I was waiting for was a bed. This seemed to take years and years but, on the 23rd February 2016, I was informed I would be moving the next day to Wales at noon.

FIRST IMPRESSIONS

I arrived early afternoon to my new rehab. It was a beautiful looking place with a grade two listed building and plenty of grounds to walk around. I didn't exactly arrive in style and instead arrived in yet another ambulance with one of my members of staff. The journey there was ok though I was nervous as hell. I mean:

What happen if they didn't like me?
If they didn't think I was ill?
What if I wasn't in fact ill and just wasting their time?

It was so bloody hard to put my first step on the ground and enter my new home.

With a sigh and a tear rolling down my face I entered the building. The staff there were really nice and on first impressions, I was quite impressed. Julie, my old staff member and I sat down and had a coffee whist the new staff unloaded my things and went through some paper work with me. Overall it all went rather quickly, from me taking my first step out of the ambulance to being led up stairs to the new ward and my new home.

The first couple of weeks were hard as I was trying to find my feet again. The ward was basically one room with a little corridor leading off it where the bedrooms were. It was nicely decorated, and I quickly claimed a seat and started to get comfortable. Days went by quite quickly even though there wasn't much to do. I found I was filling my days with arts and crafts and doing a hell of a lot of writing. My mood seemed to have settled out, which I thought, would. You see the thing with me is I settle quite quickly into new places on the exterior but on the inside, I am bricking it. I know my pattern. I was aware what would happen. That I would feel good for the first couple of weeks blocking things out and then it would crumble down. And this is exactly what happened,

Protection, mood in the weather

Blue sky of peacefulness
Is all I want to see
Yet with the sun and rain on either side
There is a fight within me

Weather can bring happiness
And never ending fun
The feeling of being invisible
As you dance into with the sun

The suns heat is so incredible
That you're unable to regain control
You're quickly burnt and soldered
As the intensity takes hold

You're running around the town
Spending everything you've earnt
The happiness and glory
Soon turns into hurt

As you realise you can't stop
You haven't stopped for days
For times like this you're with the sun
And can't see any other way

Days or weeks can carry on
Whilst you're flying with the birds
But you soon return to the mellow party of life
And appreciate what you're learnt

Yet this time is now in the pass
You've got blue skies ahead
You dissociate from what you've been through
And instead start living again

Unfortunately, it is not long
Till the clouds start coming in
Smothering your world completely
There is no life to be seen

You slowly become drowned
By everything you need to do
Everything so much effort
But the clouds keep coming though

The rain starts pouring
And your tears being to fall
Everything so difficult because
You're not so incredible anymore

Life becomes hard
It all becomes very difficult
But luckily though the rain
You find a little miracle

You find you make it through
You fight through each day
And quickly the rain
Becomes the sun again

MY TIME IN WALES

My weather and normality didn't last long. Soon I was back to cycling through the tormenting weather as it hit me with full force. I enjoyed the few weeks of 'normality' even if it was false and unconsciously placed upon me. But soon the clouds started coming in or the sun started fading out. In my low states I would cry so much and just start to isolate myself from people. I became very paranoid.

SNIPPET - PARANOID WRITING FROM PHONE

They're conspiring against me. I know they are. They're blaming me for being in pain. They don't believe me. They think I'm making it all up. They're keeping me trapped for no reason. I am literally going to die in this place. They're twisting everything around to say it's my fault. They're putting the blame on me saying I'm putting it on and twisting everything that I say. Everything I do is misinterpreted. They're conspiring against me. They don't want me here and are making it very known. They know it's increasing my pain but they carry on. They're tricking me. I know I want help, I know I need help but they are conspiring to keep me in pain. I can't even ask for pain relief because they say it's my fault. I feel so embarrassed that I stay in pain. I'm in quite a lot of pain but they think it's not hurting. I get told to act happy and normal so I do and my emotional pain increases. They do not care. They enforce it, put me down, blame me if I don't join in but the more I act normal and happy the more physical and emotional pain I'm in. They seem to like that, like to watch me suffer. They are conspiring against me. Plotting against me to make me stay in pain and remain on my own. I can't ask for PRN because I'm clearly not in as much pain as everyone else. I can't ask for paracetamol because it's clearly in my head. And I'm not allowed to cry because apparently its weak and doesn't make me happy like I should be. It's my fault because I'm not joining in. But if I join in then the pain gets intense. It doesn't go, it just blocks out for a bit then gets worse. I don't think they understand that. The more I go to group and join in the more I think that if I try and it doesn't work then I can kill myself on my date. But if I don't try then I can't reason with myself to actually go through it. Better the devil you know.

SWAP...

When the sun finally came out again, my thought pattern turned to the complete opposite. I found sleeping hard and reluctantly found myself in a non-sleeping cycle. I was spending a lot of money. For example, I bought a £3,500 course in psychology and a £350 weighted blanket. Firstly, the course was far too unsuitable for me and when I came back down I realised that, fortunately I got my psychiatrist to write a letter to the online company saying I was too ill to complete it. It was not until two months later that I got a response and they refunded the money. I count myself lucky this time!

Secondly, when the weighted blanket came it was the size of a double bed and so heavy. I couldn't believe how unsuitable it was. It wasn't till I came down from my hyper manic state that I realised how mad these ideas and shopping was. I sent back my blanket and again got a refund, however all the other things I bought I just had to live with. Over all I spent about £5000 in just over two weeks.

Summers wish

The darkness has gone
The sun has appeared
All my hurt and loneliness
Has now disappeared

I'm flying with the birds
High in the sky
Looking down on the world
Happy I survived

Survived through the dark
When crippled in pain
Survived through the storms
When covered in rain

Milly Jones

I am now sailing
Happy and free
Because I know there is a warrior
Deep inside me

TWO MONTHS IN

As I said the first few months flew by, soon I was laughing and joking with all the staff and all the patients. I was starting to develop some good friendships. My mood seemed to be settling down however my dissociation was not.

Although, my symptoms were rearing their ugly head again, I was feeling comfortable in Wales. I now had local leave with two members of staff and was off one to one most of the time (level three obs) apart from in my bedroom and at night to keep me safe. My self-harming still wasn't getting better though and I ended up in A&E with a rather bad cut on my arm.

I can't particularly say I was mended, fixed as suicidal thoughts never left my head. On one particular day I had a hospital appointment local to my home. All I kept thinking was this my chance. So I planned and planned until my plan would be successful. On the day I dressed in two sets of clothes and took my driving license and money with me. I was ready, ready to die. I had it set out of how I would run, how I knew this town more than they did so I had the upper hand. Unfortunately it was not meant to be. My arm had gotten pretty horrible of the last few days and so I was informed I had to visit A&E to get it fixed/ seen to. So regrettably my plans went out the window. I was gutted. I remain calmed and peaceful in hospital but when I got back I just broke down. This was supposed to be my day. I had had it planned for ages.... But fate stepped in my way I guess.

So the hours passed and the days ticked by but nothing seemed to be moving. I hadn't seen a psychologist yet and everything just seemed a bit odd. One morning in April the big boss man came in and sat all us patients down.

'WE ARE CLOSING!'

The words hit me like a tonne of bricks. Everyone around me, other patients, were crying and asking questions but I just froze. I couldn't find any words. I had only been there two months, and it was already a big upheaval happening. Why would they have accepted me if they knew it was going to close. It was mean. After the big boss man finished talking, I got straight onto the phone with my care coordinate.

Upsettingly so, she didn't know anything about it and she was as shocked as me. We both were thrown into a whirlwind not knowing what to do for the best. We quickly started coming up with a plan of action.

> We needed to find somewhere quickly
> It needed to be a suitable placement
> I needed to gain funding again
> I needed somewhere to stay in the mean time.

After a day or two more detail started coming out about the close. I was allowed to stay in Wales until the 16th May and then I would have to get moved to another hospital if a rehab placement didn't come up. My care coordinator and I quickly started routing around for another placement, luckily it had only been a few months ago that I had been assessed by two others places so I was in a better position than other patients. My care co got in touch with a new placement in another locked unit and we quickly got the ball rolling again.

The last month in Wales was horrible. Everyone was finding it difficult to cope and a lot of people were kicking off which made it harder on the rest of us. I couldn't wait to get out of the place. I mean I was enjoying it there and the staff were amazing but the atmosphere was that of a funeral.

To be fair most of the patients had been there for 2 years or longer. They were finding it more difficult to leave because of the attachment. Whereas I was finding it hard because honestly I was pissed off. Pissed off that they had lead me here under false pretences.

So the next month dragged, slow and long. However, we were able to go out on the last weekend we were there. At the start of May I got a call off my care coordinator saying I had been accepted into a new locked unit rehabilitation placement. This was brilliant however unfortunately they didn't have a bed for 6 - 8 weeks so I would have to look for another hospital placement in the mean time.

During the last week the patient number dwindled and for our last weekend there were just two patients left, the lady and I were able to go out discovering Wales with the staff. We got chips and ice cream and sunbathed and had a water fight. It was a brilliant weekend but still at the back of my mind I was struggling to cope. It's a horrible feeling when things are out of our hands. Out of your control. I was finding the anticipation of not knowing where I was going the next day hard to deal with. But I kept a brave face and joined in with everything

MAY 16TH 2016

D- day. I was glued to my phone. Sat waiting for my care coordinator to ring, I could be going anywhere in England. I had my fingers crossed; we all had our fingers crossed that I would get placed at The Whales in again,

9 am - nothing
10 am - nothing
11 am - nothing
12 pm - nothing
13 pm - nothing
14 pm - phone call

THE WHALE IN

Sad and excited I got my things packed and loaded them in to van. We were off within the hour, teary and nervous I had no choice. I was still under section so I had to go. I'm going back for my 5th stay...This time it wasn't my fault and that's all I kept repeating on the drive back to Blackpool.

BACK TO THE WHALES IN...A BLOG POST

OK, it's time to write. I haven't written in over a month, since I found out about the closure of Wales. I guess I was upset and heartbroken that the place that I was going to move my life forward in had to come to a quick short end.

I had survived a very rocky 3 months in Wales and all I can say is I met some fantastic people who really helped me start to develop and become more open.

Unfortunately, I have had to move back to my old local acute hospital now where luckily everyone has been brilliant and been so inviting. The staff keep reassuring me it isn't my fault that I'm back and it's completely due to circumstances out of my control. Although this is hard to hear, I know that they are right. I feel like it's a step backwards but I'm trying ever so hard to not listen to the voices in my head and instead see this as a stepping stone to getting to the next rehab.

It going to be blooming hard to take that step, that dive into the unknown again but because of the amazing staff here and the amazing staff in Wales I think I have made strong links to good experiences to make the transition easier.

ENTERING THE WHALES IN

Day one, I was transferred back to hospital, entering the building for the 5th time. I was terrified and upset at going back and with each step my legs got wobblier and my tears came faster. I was soon on the ward red faced yet trying to be brave. As soon as I stepped though the door some arms were flung around me. It was my red head friend from old hospital admissions. It was great to see her and I really appreciated her welcome. I sat down with her whilst my things were handed over. She helped calm me down and feel so much better. I hugged the staff from Wales when they left and after that I don't really understand or remember.

Day two, Woke up in a familiar yet uncomfortable surrounding. My mood had been lowering for quite a while and I could feel the fall happening. Unfortunately I ended up cutting myself rather badly and needing stitches. Luckily I didn't have to go to A&E as the doctor stitched me there. I wasn't in a good place at all but I was trying,

Poem... falling down...don't let me go

I seem to be falling
Falling out of the sky
My blue sky is going
But I just don't know why

Why is my mood dropping
What did I do wrong
Nothing has happened
Just the voices are getting strong

Did I do something to cause it
Is it all my fault
Can I do something to stop it
To ground it to a halt

It's like someone has switched off
A chemical inside
That it's stopped my brain functioning
But can I survive

My head, it feels numb
I'm left lost and scared
Of what's round the next corner
And what's waiting for me there

The dark path that follows
Is not something I want to take
Where my indentation of rain
Is waiting in my wake

I want to keep my blue skies
Because I don't know how to cope
With the darkness that's coming in
Depressing all my hope

But I'm going to hold on
As hard as I might
And not let the rain
Destroy all my fight

Day three, I cut again, I had stitches again, I struggled again.

Day four, I cut again, I had stitches again, I struggled again, I was placed on level three (one to one) observations.

Day five and onward, From the 19th of May until the 20th June I remained on level three, it was hard. I was watched having a shower, embarrassing. I was watched having a poo, embarrassing, I was watched doing anything - embarrassing. Overall it was hard because I didn't exactly want to be safe so being kept under watch all the time was hard. I was there in the Underwood for a total of 5 weeks. I made some friends, I cried a river and I laughed a rainbow. It was nice being with the amazing staff again but it was also hard because I felt I had failed then. They reassured me I hadn't and were so kind and thoughtful. Although I felt comfortable there, I needing to move on and get to my next rehab. I was on one to one obs for the entire five weeks.

KEEPING BUSY

Whilst I was in hospital, my friends and family were able to visit much more which was brilliant. I realised whilst in hospital how much my parents help me and are amazing. So instead of cutting one night, with tremendous effort, my favourite support worker (who was with me) encouraged me to write something to them.

I decided to write a poem....

To my parents... a poem to express things I can not say

You help me through the rain,
When my mood is low
You help me through the pain,
When I can't carry on

For this I thank you

You help me feel the sun,
And help me when it's starting to burn
When my high has turned nasty,
You come and calm my world

For this I thank you

You stand by my side,
Whilst I struggle to cope
You give me a chance to talk
To fill me with hope

Milly Jones

For this I thank you

You pull me up
When I'm starting to fall
Holding me tight
Whenever I call

For this I thank you

You listen to me speak
When I say I am fine
You give me comfort
By soothing my mind

For this I thank you

You open your ears
Open your heart
Allows me to have the strength to fall apart

For this I thank you

You have loved me unconditionally all my life
Yet I find it hard to express
My feelings in this fight

For this I say thank you

This is a thank you to my parents
Who are amazingly strong
My parents that mean the world to me
Who ultimately make me carry on

I find it hard to tell my parents I love them but really I do.

MOVE NUMBER SEVEN

On the 17th of June I was told yet again that another place had a new bed available for me at my third rehab unit – Oak hospital. Again I was scared and excited but within Oak hospital came a new chance, a new yellow brick road to follow.

OAK HOSPITAL – IS THIS MY LAST CHANCE?

I arrived at Oak hospital yet again in a rather uncomfortable style. This time I had two members of staff sat either side of me in the back seat of a very small taxi and my care coordinator in the front. A very scary looking crew came out of the building and gathered my things then shimmied me out of the car. I was patted down and my stuff examined as I sat in the family room with my staff. The motley looking crew were fantastic and very friendly. They offered drinks and tried to make me feel at ease in a very uneasy situation.

I was soon shown to my ward and to my room. The ward looked a lot more like The Whales in than Wales and was much bigger. My room was pretty with a nice window that looks into the garden. I slowly unpacked my things whilst my staff handed things over to the new staff. Everyone seemed very pleasant and I felt a little safer which was good.

I can't really remember my first night but I settled in quite fast, I was placed on level 4 observations which meant that staff had to be within a hands reach of me at all times. This I was used to because it had been the same the five weeks I was at The Whales in.

My first few weeks flew by yet my voices were becoming a real issues. I still had many open cuts on my arms that I kept re-opening due to their commands.

THE VOICES...

Imagine you're walking down the street to buy some milk, suddenly out of nowhere someone shouts, "Hey fatty, how ugly are you?" Unfortunately, you will instantly remember that voiced comment over any other thought patterns going on in your head. That's my experience of hearing voices.

To me, I feel like for a period of time my personality and soul are stolen from me. All that makes me me is destroyed and taken away by these horrible chanting, derogatory, threatening voices. I lose contact with reality and am forced to keep one foot in death rather than to engage with the living. I follow the commands of the voices, acting on self-harm and suicide plans that are being chanted. All the creative coping mechanisms go out the window, all known survival technique are ripped from my head and instead replaced with inner turmoil as my brain tries to get used to the abuse it's receiving. I rip at my hair, scratch my hands, do anything to try and stop me from acting over the vision I see before me. I hallucinate cuts, deep cuts on my arms and commanding voices telling me where to self-harm. The urges, the voices are so strong threatening me to do it. The temptation is so strong that I can physically feel ligatures around my neck and blades sliding against my skin. For in this moment I lose touch with reality. Voices take away my soul, my heartbeat. They make me think a certain way, behave a certain way which is inevitably destroying my life.

The battle of battles between me and my voices

I feel like a superhero
Ready to fly
That my golden wings are ready
To head to the bright blue sky

"But I have adopted you,
The devil's hand in yours,
A thunderstorm of tormenting words
Means I will be with you forever more"

Right now I feel strong
Positive and free
Like I can lift from this life
And finally be me

"Yet I rise like a beast
And take over your soul
My power is so incredible
You will be forced to lose control"

I know I have the strength
It's all buried inside
I am a superhero after all
I just can't wait to take flight

"I will torture you to your knees
Turn you into a quivering wreck
As my twisted power of innocence
Makes you wish you were truly dead"

Every day I feel happy
Caught up with the sun
My golden wings sparkle
I'm grateful the life I've won

"Yet my voice is loud as thunder
Whipping through your brain
I will destroy every inch of your body
Making your life difficult to explain"

So I am strong and free
I am excited for that flight
To fly each and every day
Whilst I'm living my lovely life

"The truth you hear is incredibly
Conjured up from my soul
Although its nasty, mean, its very real
My words they will take control"

I'm determined to prove
If only to myself
That if I try hard enough
My life will become the best

"My fiery commands will crusade through your bones
Burning you alive
As I am in my hiding place
Forever and always it is your mind"

MY OUTLOOK FOR REHAB THREE

I want to learn to like myself. I don't want to listen to the voices created from my head and the lies they tell. It's so hard to try and move on. I want to talk about what people say to me what running commentary I have going on in my head. How everyday l don't believe what I think and have to force the voices to shut up to function. I am trying so hard to move my life on and try and force the evil voices away. But as I do, I am reminded by my seizures and loss of voice that just aggravates my voices further. I guess I want to talk about things that I can't let out. I feel I have so many secrets that I can't tell in my head, never mind out loud. I hate myself so much that I don't even want to get better. It feels so painful to admit. I hate that nothing has gone wrong to cause this. That there was no childhood trauma that would make it understandable. I HATE that I think that. I would love to have the feeling that I wanted to live and that I didn't have a suicide plan all the time. I like who I can be sometimes but it's like I am two separate people. One who everyone else can see and one who is intertwined with a huge pain.

How do I take away the pain, the voices? I'm fighting so hard to gain a normal life but it feels too far away. It's like I said to Dr Candy, it's like going on a Bear Hunt and I have to move all the other people and things out my head. The happy ones that want to play all the time and stay up all night. And the dark voices who want to hide. Lithium helps me fight the battle but my brain is all muddled of how to stay stable. I want more than anything to stay stable and am battling so hard. l want to talk about my fear of getting better, my hate of myself and my seizures. I want to know what make things so hard and why I am finding it so hard to process things. I really am trying my best to move on and get to OT next year but will someone please tell my head that!

LIFE ON THE WARD

After a few weeks I began to get used to the ward and the beautiful patients it had in it. They all had their own district personality traits and, over the next two months we really bonded and life was becoming bearable again. I start creating a "Positivity book" in my bedroom. It had pages with information about me, my likes and dislikes, my short and long terms goals, what I wanted in life. And anything positive that was encouraging me to get better.

I showed it to some of my new friends and they loved it. Quickly it became the new fashion trend. Everyone was making one, it was fantastic a really uplifting experience. I loved that I was using my Occupational Therapy skills again. This really did empower me and built up some self esteem, even if only a tiny bit.

In August we were allowed to decorate the ward walls. I drew two large pictures on the wall of the foyer as you walk into the ward. One was of a tree with birds flying from it. On it was a quote saying:

"Breathe little one,
You can fly,
Out of your cage,
Up to the sky,"

The second picture was of an ash tree leaf and the wards name with the quote:

"The ash tree grows tall and mighty,
Feeding from the ground,
Together we need to find our roots,
In order to survive".

Again I was empowered "I drew the tree." I drew the welcome sign and I made up the quotes. But what's more everyone joined in helping. We all painted at least a little bit and had a great laugh doing so; it was great to build up new friendships. Personally I found using my occupational therapy skills enhanced me again thus helping me tremendously.

A LETTER TO MYSELF

Dear Milly,

This is a letter, a letter to yourself. I am just writing this letter to say –
you are doing great!

You are finally on the track of recovery and it's great that you are
moving forwards. I am so proud of you. You need to keep going onwards
and upwards. Please stop listening to those nasty voices and start respecting
your body. You do not need the scars, you do not need the pain or hurt,
you deserve a life where you live it to the fullest and become everything
that you want and deserve to be. The voices do not control you; there is
no need to act on what they say. I believe in you. I do believe you will get
better and become everything you want to be. I know right now you are
finding it hard to see this, to take onboard any of this information or the
truth. But one day you will. One day you will see a light, a light so bright
at the end of your tunnel that it will put the sun to shame. I believe in you
and so do hundreds of other people. Do it for them but moreover ... *DO
IT FOR YOURSELF*

Your sincerely,
Milly Jones   (19/07/2016)

THE TURN AROUND

It was on a bleak Thursday afternoon in August that my pulse starting beating again. It wasn't particularly dramatic or strong but it was enough to know I was missing life. I was missing being a part of something bigger, of living instead of just surviving. I had been on Clozaril for 4 days so it could be that it was working as a placebo or that I was just generally in a great mood. I started to reflect back on the times I used to spend with mum going out for coffee and shopping. I could see it happening but it was so far away. I sat there in the quiet room with pictures spinning round my head like they do in movies.

- My mum and coffee
- My friend and partying
- My friends at university
- Walking my dog

<u>Freedom</u>

I knew right then that I needed to break out of this system and start living. So I came up with a plan:

<u>A discharge plan</u>

<u>September</u> - local leave

          unescorted grounds leave

          Off Level 3 in bedroom

<u>October</u>- Local town leave

<u>November</u>- Home leave - escorted firstly – early November

unescorted – late November with parents

<u>December</u> - Over night leave for - 5th December - my birthday
           - Christmas

<u>January</u> - Increase home leave

<u>February</u> - Unescorted leave everywhere

<u>March / April</u> – Discharged

That was my planning when going into my CPA on the 15th of August,

CPA – CARE PROGRAM APPROACH MEETING

9.30am on the dot my care coordinator and father arrived and met me on the ward. I was rather nervous and kept talking to my dad about my worries and concerns. My care coordinator went into the CPA first to discus how well I was coping and future plans. My father and I were invited in after half an hour. I sat down nervously on the chair. My doctor was really nice and helped me to talk about my problems. They gave an overview of what they had discussed and said that my discharge plan was a really good idea and something that is reasonable to stick to. It may take a few more months if I have a dip but I am excited that I maybe out by next April, 2017. He then asked if I had any questions, and I had one burning one. My Diagnosis. I bought it up and he said he would talk about it in a separate meeting. Other than that I didn't have much more to discuss. I was doing well and coping. The voices were getting less, as the Clozaril was being increased. All I could say was that I was fighting, fighting a hard battle against myself.

Fight the urge... fighting the voices

    This is a poem
A poem to myself
To stop hurting my body
And look after my health

It's so hard to keep fighting
Each and every day
With the voices that control me
Derogatory in what they say

They make me twist and turn
Shiver in tremendous pain
They surge though my body
Making my arms difficult to explain

So sometimes I give in
I act on their commands
I cut my skin to bits
Making me fall into their plans

I hate myself for doing this
I feel guilty, hurt and upset
For this is one moment in time
That I will sadly regret

But this is new
This feeling of dispair
Because once I didn't give a Damn
But now I actually care

I don't want anymore scars
I don't want anymore cuts
I don't want anymore regerts
And I don't want anymore blood

I don't want to feel
Like I have let myself down
Each time I hear the voices
Or act on their nasty commands

I need to take control
I should not be afaird
I need to stop hurting myself
And stop living in such great pain

I may make mistakes
Even two or three
But the fact that I want to change
Is all I need to believe

MONTHS TICKED ON

Days and weeks dragged on and I seem to have plateaued. I was still stuck in a self-harm circle of getting stitches then not letting the wound heal. My arms were still a mess, the voices were quieter but my head was still up in space somewhere arguing with some invisible voice.

In early November it was decided that I move wards as I was seen as progressing. Many staff disagreed with this move, especially my name nurse. But hey ho it happened, and it was extremely hard. My plateau was destroyed and I was left struggling again. I got placed on level 3 observations again (Eye sight at all times) and was desperately trying to hurt myself. I calmed down after a few weeks, the staff seemed nice and so did the girls, the problem was just me. I felt a lot more lonely on this new ward though I still joined in with everything and got on with everyone. Things started to develop quickly and I soon got my home leave back, slowly building up to staying nights. Looking back I feel I was pushed too quickly back into the community. I used to either steal things from home or cut myself whilst I was there. No one checked so it went on for quite a while. Although i got on with the staff and patient I still felt the same – sad, lonely and very suicidal.

Fortunately, looking back now my behaviour summed up the rehab and how I was managing. I was on my home leave for a weekend with my parents. I was enjoying it, the voices were a lot less but the urges strong. I had planned my next move for weeks and no one was going to stop me.

Saturday –Plan number 1 was in the bath. Crimson red water circled my body I could see the demons being released through a long zigzag cut on my left arm. I knew it needed stitches, but it would have to wait.

Sunday – Plan number 2 was in the shower. Trickling down my body the red water hugged my legs and disappeared down the plug. It didn't hang around but as I cut deeper the flesh opened and my body finally felt calm again. I was free until next time.

Unfortunately, the second cut had gone a bit too deep. Having had infection after infection I thought it best to get it seen to. Sheeply, I headed down the stairs to see my mum. What an amazing person she is. I know I would hate to see anyone doing this to themselves, its so hard to understand. Never mind your own daughter.

However she gave a hug, we got ready and headed for A&E. My dad wasn't too surprised but was also very supportive.

A&E were great as always. Unfortunately, this time they had to contact my rehab. They made my mum promise to take me back. That wasn't in the plan. I didn't want to go back, but reluctantly I did. I was place on 1.1 for a week after that.

CARE – COORDINATOR

Through the past few months my care coordinator had being getting updates of how I was doing and checking that this rehab was right for me. Obviously, things weren't going well and I wasn't processing as good as we thought or needed. She came to see one morning in March and we had a discussion about where things were going. Apparently, my rehab thought I was close to discharge even though I was still self-harming and expressing suicidal thoughts and plans. The psychologist there was brilliant, but they wanted to set up some psychologist in the community. This didn't seem to make much sense. So she asked me if I want to stay or wanted to see if we could find somewhere more suitable.

I couldn't believe it, all the energy, paperwork, waiting and finding somewhere. It was a huge deal to undertake but we both decided that moving was the right thing to do. So we got looking and luckily my care coordinator had a colleague who had someone in a Pinewood Hospital in North East England. It was a long way away but sounded a lot better and more suitable for my needs. Soon the ball was rolling and I had an assessment and was accepted. The staff were nice in my last weeks there. I was stable ish but I had no idea what new world I was entering into. It will either be the death of me or the making. Fingers crossed, I wasn't quite sure which I preferred.

PINEWOOD HOSPITAL

15th of May 2017 came around rather quickly in the end. I had so many things to take with me. It is surprising how much stuff you collect in hospital. I had already sent lots home with my parents a couple of weeks before but it was still piled high in my bedroom. It was my named nurse and a male HCA who drove the three hours up North. I was able to sit in the front so didn't feel as sick which was much appreciated. We stopped for a McDonald's on the way that made a nice break. The journey went rather quickly overall, but with each ticking mile on the clock the more nervous I became.

Finally we arrived late in the afternoon. The hospital looked lovely with extensive grounds, rabbits running round and squirrels. I was admitted to Rose ward. I was terrified walking in with my named nurse to strange surroundings. Everyone greeted me nicely as I was lead to a small room just off the main lounge. An new nurse called Eva came in and greeted herself to my old named nurse and myself. She seemed nice and the handover was quick and painless. It all seemed to fly by and before I knew it my old team were gone and I was being shown to my new bedroom. All the bedrooms I have been in are all very much the same. I slowly unpacked, not wanting to unpack everything straight away.

- How long would I be staying?
- Can they help e, cure me?

Is time slipping away?

I held my breath, walked in the communal area and sat down.

Rose ward was the complete the opposite to the previous Rehab ward. They moved everything at a slower rate and really included me in every step they took. I quickly made friends and my observations started on 1 to 1 and decreased slowly to half an hours. Over the time I was there I only ended up in A&E once for staples. My Self-harm had reduced dramatically in just a few short months. At the time of writing I have been 114 days self harm free. (24/09/17). To celebrate my hundred days self harm free I bought myself a Pandora owl charm.

This became my new way to cope with self-harm

A ROLLERCOASTER RIDE THAT'S GUAR

Self harm

As mentioned I used to self harm because of the voices and the hallucinations. Fortunately, Clozaril had made these symptoms slowly disappear. However, even deep down the urges to still self-harm hadn't gone, I was starting to discover my triggers. I found that now I wasn't getting told where, when or how-to Self-harm decreased the urges. So, the planning changed. I decided to get artistic to show my progress and put my planning to another use. I began feeling the like the old me. My pulse was finally returning, like when I went to Canada. Everything about life was starting to feel real. The demons were hushed, and my soul was back. It was amazing, something I can't put into words. I have a new outlook on life. As the days, weeks and months ticked by I become more and more confident and expressive.

My survival pathway

1. My First Stop Self-harming plan

Travel money – My brother lives in Canada with my niece and nephew. I would love to either fly out to see him and his family OR meet them somewhere else; like Thailand. So every day I don't self-harm I put a shiny new pound coin. (Ironically, they all very shinny and the new pound coins have just been released in 2017)

2. <u>Positivity Book</u>

Using blank cards that I stuck together I decided to create a book - all about me. It has my symptoms, likes, dislikes, goals and everything that is positive about staying alive and keeping away from Self Harming. (Mentioned in above text)

3. <u>Discharge Ladder</u>

Using the months of the year I made a ladder by my bed sticking stickers on each day I don't self-harm. I also started tracking my weight for when I started slim fast.

4. <u>My Tree</u>

This is my second favourite piece of art. My consultant loves it and says I should get it patented, so that it can't be copied. I have made an outline of a tree in beautiful decorative tape and placed flowers and leaves on it. I made the flowers out of medication pots. I did bigger flowers that had Velcro on them so you could move little wooden animals around depending on your situation at the time. For example – days of self harm 50,100,150,200.

<u>Finally finding who I am...</u>

On 6th November 2017 I finally came out. I admitted to my parents and everyone else that I was bi-sexual.

"I have something to tell you that is really hard to say. I don't want this to change anything, as I love you all so much. I have gone over and over of how I should say this. But letting this go I will finally be free and have nothing holding me back. I still want a wedding and I still want children, but it may be with a girl or a boy.

It has taken a long time to finally admit who I am and I hope you can accept me. I am still daddy's little girl."

I was so nervous about telling anyone, let alone my parents. It all started when I spoke to a HCA in hospital. I admitted I like girls to her and before I knew it I was sat with the psychiatrist in ward round who said i should be happy with who i am. I shocked but moreover I was relieved. From then on most of the staff found out but nothing on the outside changed. I was still Milly but on the inside I felt completely different. I felt like a weight had been lifted from my shoulders. I felt so empowered, that with the help from staff I told my parents, i really didn't know how they were going to take it but as the words fell from my moth they didn't react. I was still their little girl. If I am happy, then they are!

From the times I remember when they sat by me, holding my hand as I got stitches or rushing me to A&E after an overdose. They stood by me through the worst of times and never gave up. My parents are amazing and I know now that they accept me as me. I feel so loved and if they can accepted me than so can I.

It's scary, it's exciting but it's my life and I cannot wait!

Discharge plan - 21/11/2017

The day came, the day to plan for my discharge, my future. For some reason I was nervous going into ward round this week. I felt a little uneasy and not myself. I guess I had no plan of what I want to talk about which had caused me to be a little more nervous than normal – how wrong could I have been.

I sat down with the psychiatrist, psychologist and a ward nurse. This meeting was being held to talk about plans for discharge and to start to plan some more leave Even though, like i have previous stated, i was scared about home leave this was a chance to talk it though and make a solid plan.... as follows.

<u>Transfer from hospital to home.</u>

My real transfer started on the 4th December 2017. I had been building up to this day for quite a while. It was going to be my last escorted leave home. I have to say I was excited about the process but also terrified. At least I learnt in DBT the two things can be true at the same time! I was terrified about the thought of being left alone and not under 24/7 support. I mean what if things get too much? If the loneliness', self-harming and suicidal idolisation came back with revenge. I want a new life so badly. I want the way I am feeling now to carry on; I am desperately praying that this 'change' in me is permanent. It's scary! I can't wait for my home leave and to follow the discharge plan, but I need to remain kind to myself.

Excited – Yes
Terrified – Yes

<u>December 2017</u>
4th – Home leave – Last escorted – seeing care coordinator - going for a early birthday dinner
18th – Home leave – First unescorted – putting up Christmas tree
27th – Home leave – Second unescorted – Mini Christmas with family

<u>January 2018</u>
7th-8th – Night home leave
14th – 15th – Night in York
22nd-23rd – Night home leave – meal out Matthews birthday

<u>February 2018</u>
3 days home leave
4 days home leave
1 week leave
Rest week

<u>March 2018</u>
2 weeks home

Rest week
4 weeks home

<u>April 2018</u>
<u>Continue 4 weeks at home</u>
23rd DISCHARGE!

<u>My weeks at home</u>

Most of my weeks at home where uneventful. Everything was going well. I was settling quite quickly in my old home. However one of my main issues that arose, well the only issues really, was around food time. I was used to very firm regimented times for having dinner at 12 and tea 5. These times don't suit my family life. Here, we have dinner between 1 and 2 and then tea at 7. At first I found this really hard because in addition to this I was usually in bed my seven. This meant that by the time it was teatime at 7 I was very tired. I guess in hospital nothing really happens after tea and everyone retreats to their bedrooms. Now being back home life goes on after tea with playing games and cards.

I thought this was going to be a major problem but as I got used to it on my two weeks leave everything just seemed to fall into place.

<u>Career</u>

Throughout the book I have been very undecided on who i would like to be, what I would like to achieve. I have floated between psychology, counselling and occupational therapy Degrees. To help decide I created a book which included the pros and cons of studying the courses and pro and con of not studying. For the top courses they were very much the same with the main aim of the course attached to a career. I then ventured further and looked at things that I enjoy which I might be able to make into career.

<u>Cake baking</u>

Something I was good at, I enjoyed, less stress, I could do short courses and good progression. However, its very competitive market and I would be starting from scratch. Things were looking good for this career but then I found out you can't sell cakes from a house where dog lives.

Back to the drawing board

I was thinking of something that would be personal to me, so the last 4 years weren't a compete waste. It would have to be not too stressful and close to home. Something achievable and exciting.

<u>Camouflage make up</u>.
Brilliant. Get rid of my scars, personal to me, and a course down the road only a 20 min walk away.
Can start in September and have a brilliant outcome. Can have a rest after discharge.
This would be building on my strengths and personality, instead of making myself into an occupational therapist or a psychologist. It's fits my life and I can arrange it all around myself. Excited.
Unfortunately, things did not flow right but I was not giving up on this yet. The course just up from where I live was not suitable. It was kind of back to the drawing board, but I didn't want to let this idea go.

<u>Starting to move on</u>
On my two weeks leave from the ward I was slowly re-entering myself back into society. The biggest thing that I didn't actually believe would happen was I got a date. *A date with a boy!*
I met him at a local pub and we stayed there talking for hours. I found him so interesting and the conversation flowed so well. It was going so well that I went with my gut and told him I was in hospital. His reply was – "You're fascinating." He couldn't understand how I could have done all this travelling and learning when I had been locked up for the previous five years.

His reaction in a way was so nice. He didn't back down or shy away. In fact we booked in another date the following week. Things are going well.

As I was getting things sorted I had to change doctors. This to most people might just be a simple action but to me it was a big deal. My doctor was amazing and used to phone me every night when I was ill at university. I decided to change as he left the surgery to go on to pastures new. I wrote this poem when he left but never got the chance to give it him. He really was my saviour.

Dear Doctor
This is a thanks
For all the things you did for me
But I never got the chance

To thank you in person
Or give you a hug
Because you have meant so much to me
And you never judged

All the letters you must have received
And referrals that you made
You always took me as me
Despite the mess I made

I loved when you asked
If my arms were behaving
To save on the embarrassment
Of my self harming adventures

You always had a chuckle
At my various diagnoses
Making jokes about your computer
Also having multiple personalities

But when things got serious
You were always there
Phoning me at univesity
And getting me the right care

Your computer drove you crazy
And your time keeping wasn't great
But sitting in that waiting room
You knew your time was well spent

Listening to everyone's problems
You took time to understand
What each person was going through
And how you could lead a hand

So some GPs have a bad name
But you were incredibly kind
You were extremely good at your job
And you definitely put in the time

You will be missed by so many
And be impossible to replace
If anyone deserves retirement
It is you, so enjoy your Break

FOUR FINAL WEEKS

I am slowly getting used to being at home and normal living. I am on my four weeks leave and things are going better then I ever expected.

Firstly, things are going well with my boyfriend. We meet 3 days a week, chatting and going for food. I love spending time in his company. He is funny and very attractive, and we just seem to click. He met my parents on the 22nd April, the night before discharge and my section being rescinded. They all got on perfectly. I can really see him in my life, but moreover I can finally see a future.

During the days of my four weeks I started volunteering for a local café. I would wait on and did the washing up. I thoroughly enjoyed it. Eventually as the weeks ticked by I started volunteering for two days.

The final piece of my jigsaw happened on Friday 13th April…. I got my driving licence back! As soon as I had the little pink card in my hand I was excited. Without delay I was searching for cars. I went from looking at Ford Fiestas, to Clio's, to finally a Mini. We looked at two in total until I fell in love. My mini is a slivery blue convertible. I drove my newly bought car home from Lancaster and finally felt free again.

23RD APRIL – THE ENDING

My father and I drove up on the last trip to Pinewood Hospital. I was so excited to say goodbye to this life. I can honestly say I cant remember what has fully happened in these last five years and that actually this book is helping me to. I signed the paper. I was discharged from hospital, off my section. A free woman.

AN END MESSAGE

This The End Poem

I never thought I would write
It's a poem of bravery
Against the fight

I was fighting against the beast
I was fighting against the power
I was fighting against myself
Nearly suffering my final hour

I came so close
To death it'sself
That I never believed
I would achieve anything else

But up I rose
Clinging on to the sight
That I will make it through
Just don't turn off the light

For I have grown
In many ways
I have learnt to love myself
And accept my pain

I no longer self harm
I no longer self loathe
Instead I enjoy my life
And everything it holds

So I love my family
I love my friends
And I will love my life
Until the end

A FINAL NOTE

I was discharged on 23rd of April 2018 from Pinewood hospital, a hospital that had changed my life. I have never felt, so happy, so free, and so grateful to be alive. Getting used to community living is a slow process and hard to get to grips with. I have an amazing man who is helping me by going out to the local pubs and restaurants instead of sending time ruminating in my room. He has been brilliant and a real rock to talk to, although he does not understand my dark path which I was lost in for years, this I am grateful for. He can always see the fun loving girl that loves him dearly.

Life is great at the moment. I am meeting up with friends I haven't seen or sometimes-even spoken to for years. I am experiencing things which I haven't done for years. I am building my confidence up, I am starting a mood-tracking course in September so psychological help isn't too far away. I have a brilliant care coordinator. My mates are amazing and my family fantastic. Finally, I am now 1 year and 2 months self harm free. I am so proud of myself and it is on wards and upwards from here.

I am now living life instead of just being on it for a ride. A rollercoaster ride!

ACKNOWLEDGMENTS

This is the first book I have ever written but it would not of been possible without help from some fanatic friends, family and professionals. Firstly, most importantly I would like to say how much I respect Michelle Wilson, a dear friend. She single handily edited this book for me and corrected my spelling and grammar. She did a fanatic job and I would like to thank you.

Second thanks goes to my parents. Reading this book has helped me see how much they have gone through and coped with my illness. I think you are both amazing people and love you both indefinably.

My final thanks goes to Rach Wright, Katherine Turner and Laura Gillespie. Rach read through my book at draft phase and encouraged me into completing this book. There would not have been a book without her. Kathryn is my best friend who I turn on for everything. She has been the best company through out the writing of this book. My home friend Laura, who I lean on in times of struggle and she helps me see the bigger picture. I thank her for always being there for me

At last, I would also like to give a huge thanks to the brilliant and fanatic work done by the NHS and private hospital staff.